SYMMETRICAL UNIVERSE

Adult Coloring Book #2

Spaceships, Machines, and Steampunk Images for
Relaxation, Inspiration, and Stress Relief

by Stephen Pitts

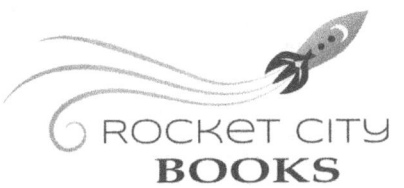

ROCKET CITY
BOOKS

www.rocketcitybooks.com

Published by Rocket City Books
PO Box 74
Taft, TN 38488
info@rocketcitybooks.com
256.714.7980
www.rocketcitybooks.com

ISBN 978-0-9903547-2-7

WELCOME!

Welcome to the Symmetrical Universe Spaceship and Steampunk coloring book! I hope you enjoy contemplating and coloring these complex images inspired by science fiction.

I drew every image in this book with pen and ink on 14x17 paper. My drawings are all done by hand, using fine tipped Rapidiograph pens. The way my process works is first I use a ruler and a compass to generate a pencil line grid. Once the grid is in place I then draw the designs in ink. The images are randomly generated and sometimes change significantly during the process of creating them. The drawings are created by drawing one symmetrical feature at a time, much like growing a crystal.

These drawings are inspired by my interest in science fiction and machinery. My drawings are also expressions of the inherent beauty found in symmetrical structures. I began drawing mandalas while attending Indian Springs School in Helena, Alabama in the 1970s. My first mandala drawings began as simple experiments requiring a few hours to design. This eventually led to the more complex designs which required 80 to 100 hours to complete. Some drawings are abstract geometrical designs. In others, I have tried to incorporate archetypical symbols and shapes similar to Rorschach patterns which may invoke a variety of conceptualizations to viewers of my artwork.

In this book, each section includes an original drawing which may be too detailed to color. The following pages are all more detailed images of sections of each drawing for you to enjoy and color. If you are interested in coloring an original drawing in the original size, order a print from www.symmetricaluniverse.com.

To get the most out of this book, I recommend using colored pencils, fine-point markers, or gel pens. Before you color on one of the drawings, use the test page on the very last page of this book to test your coloring pencils, pens, and erasers. Check to see if your pencils or pens look nice on the paper and make sure they don't bleed through to the back.

To see more of my drawings, visit my webpage at www.symmetricaluniverse.com. You may order prints of any of my drawings in a variety of sizes. You may also order my other coloring book on mandalas and symmetrical designs. Sign up for my newsletter to get updates about new drawings, new coloring books, and a schedule of my art shows.

Thank you for ordering this book. I hope you enjoy it!

Steve Pitts

See more of my drawings
and sign up for my newsletter:

www.symmetricaluniverse.com

AUGMENTED DIHEDRAL STRUCTURE

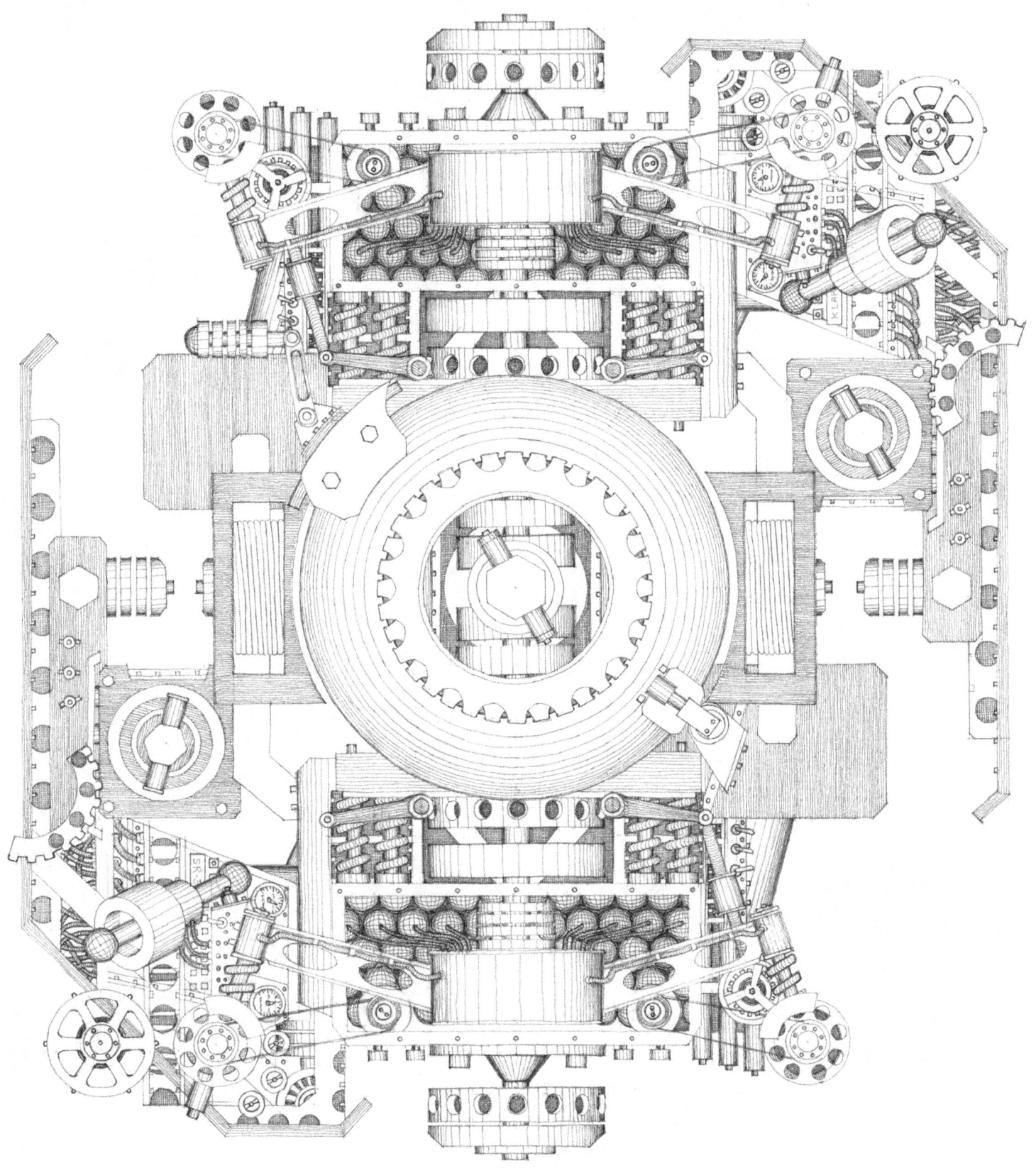

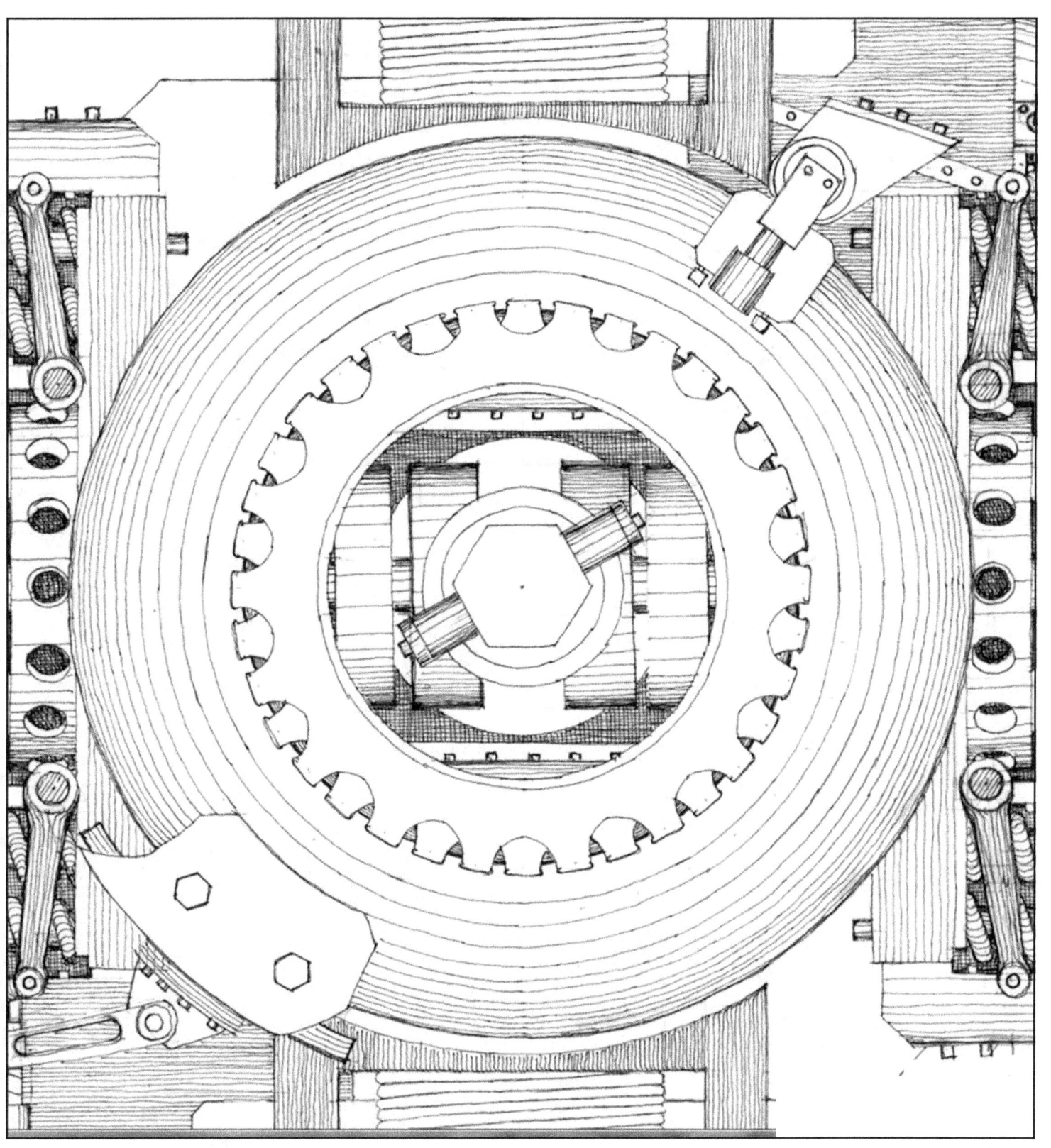

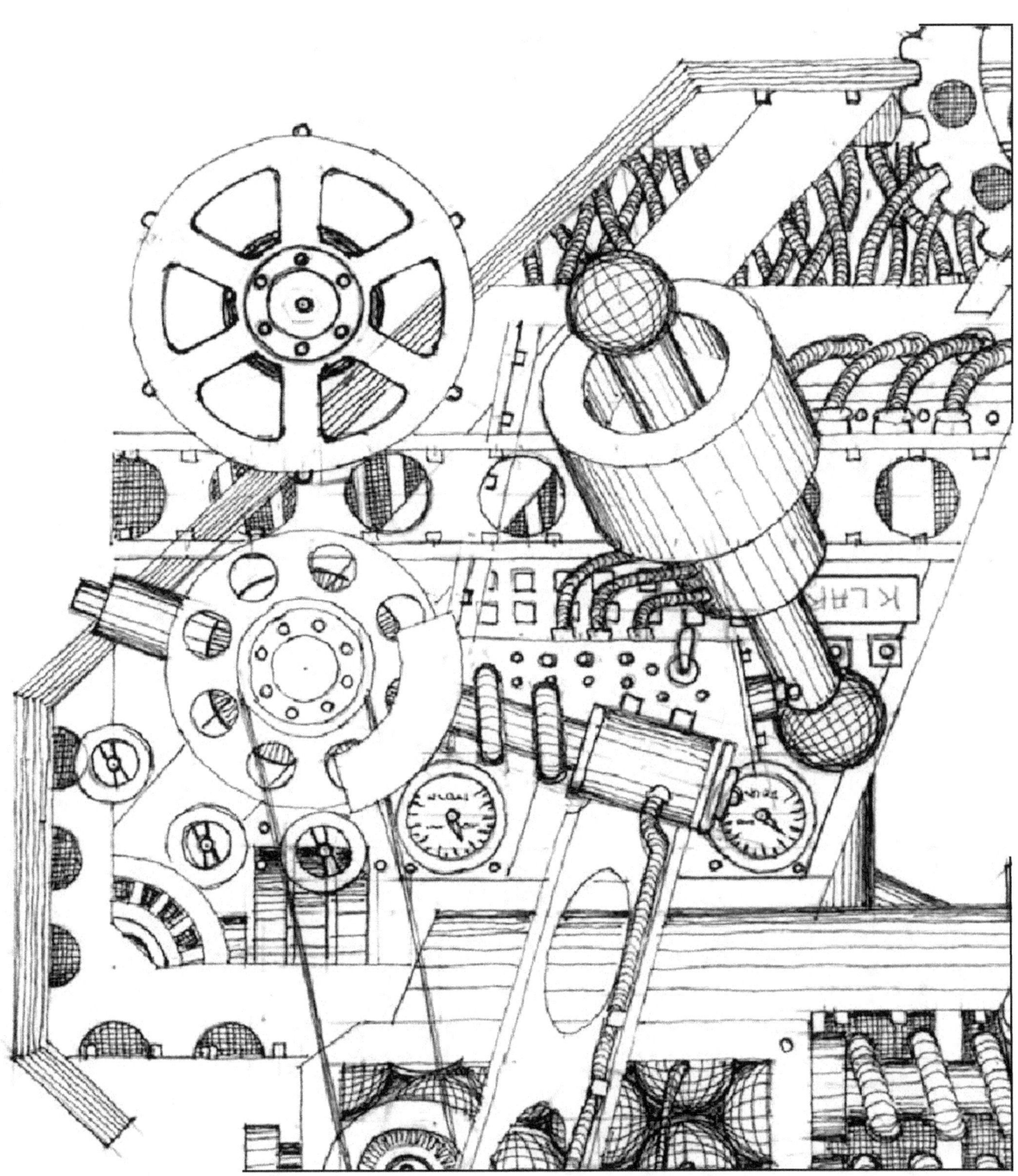

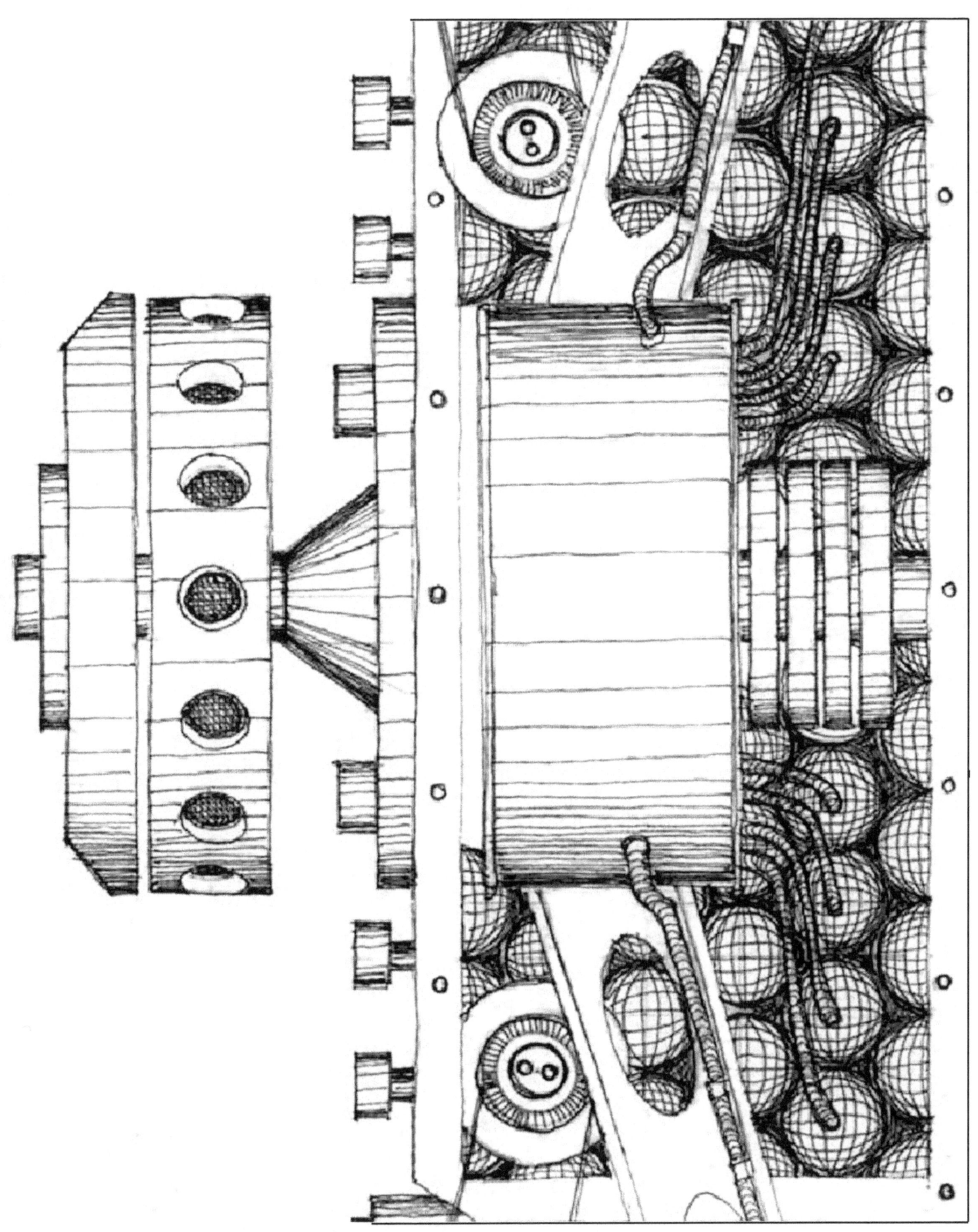

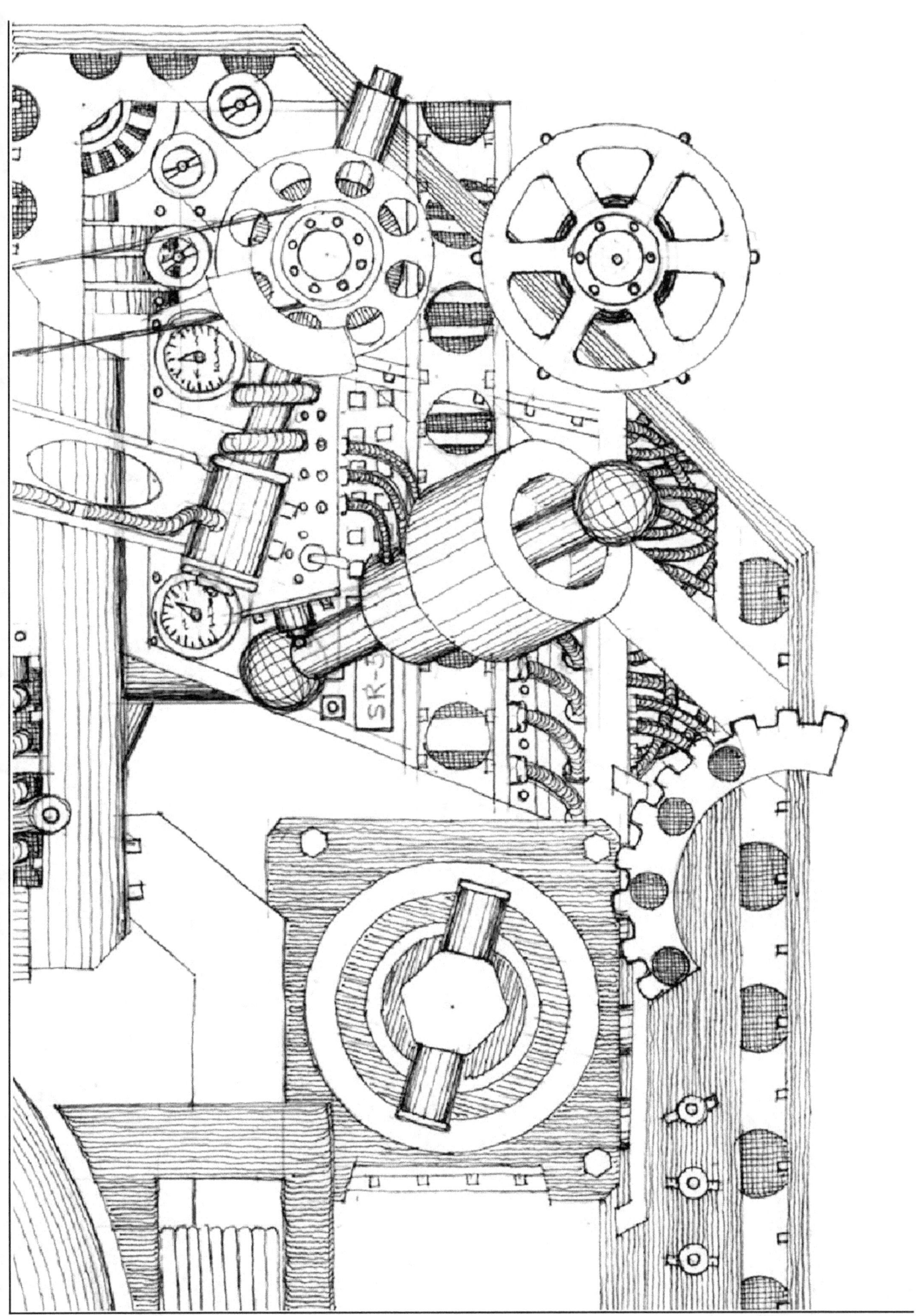

CRUSTACEAN

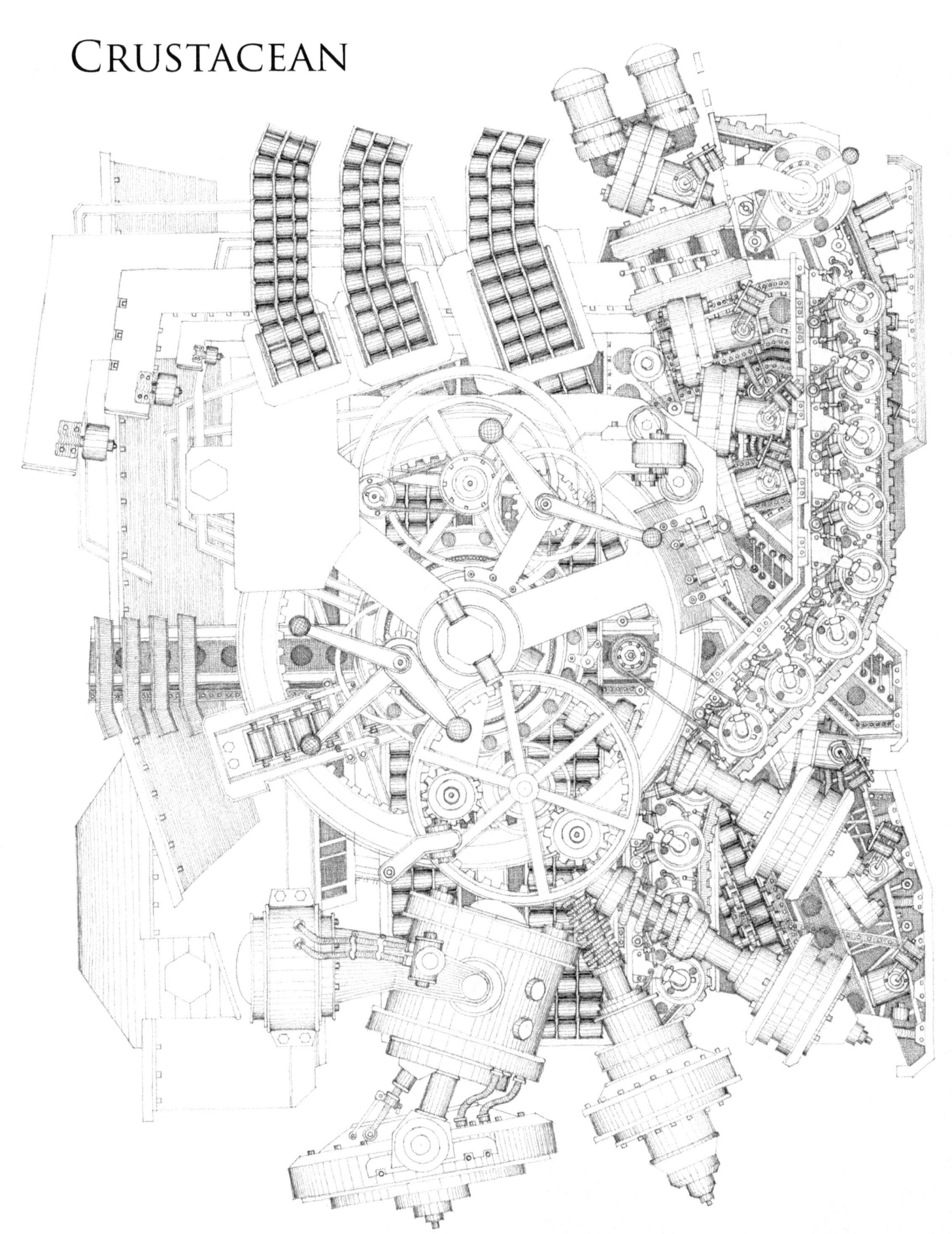

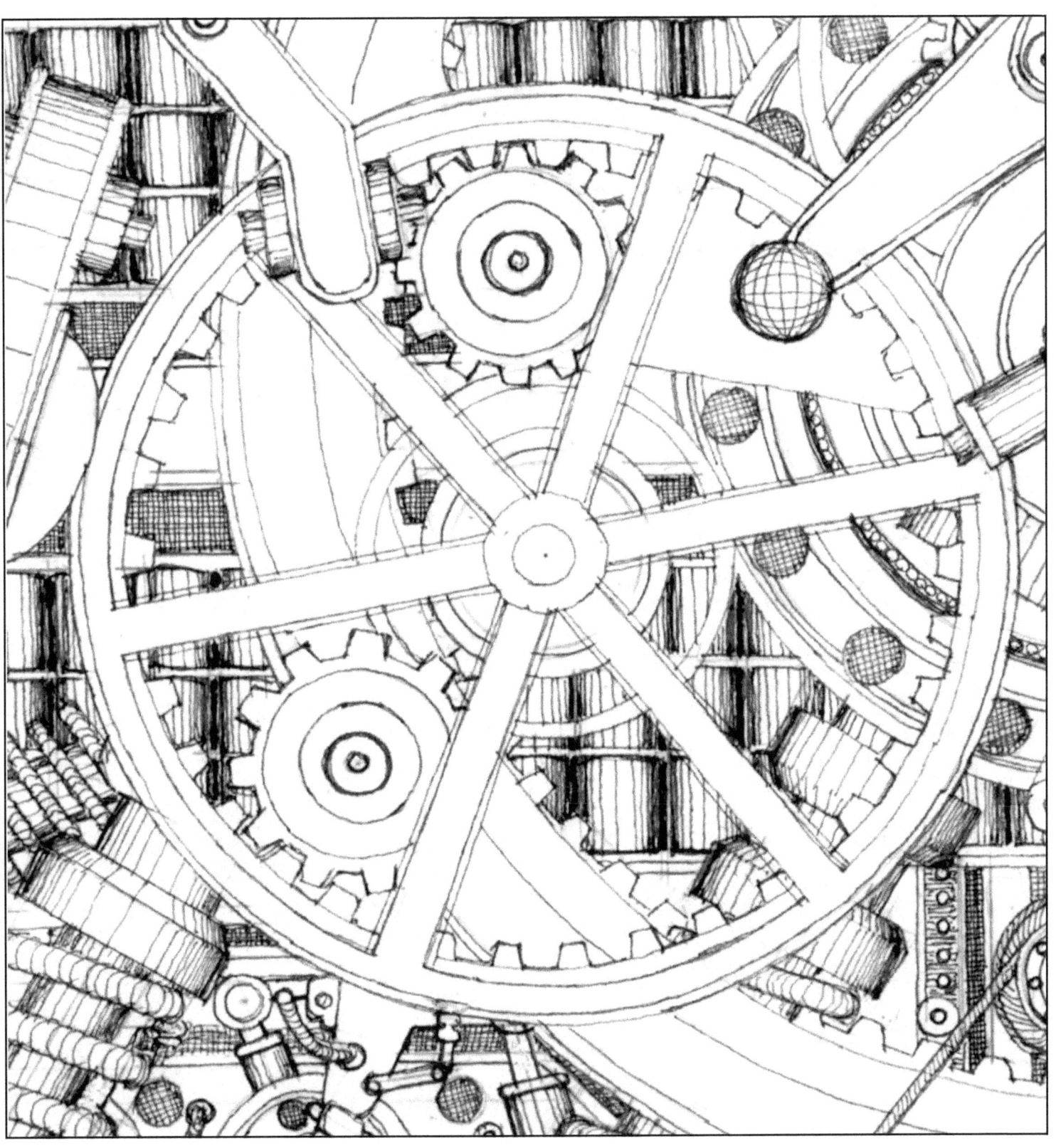

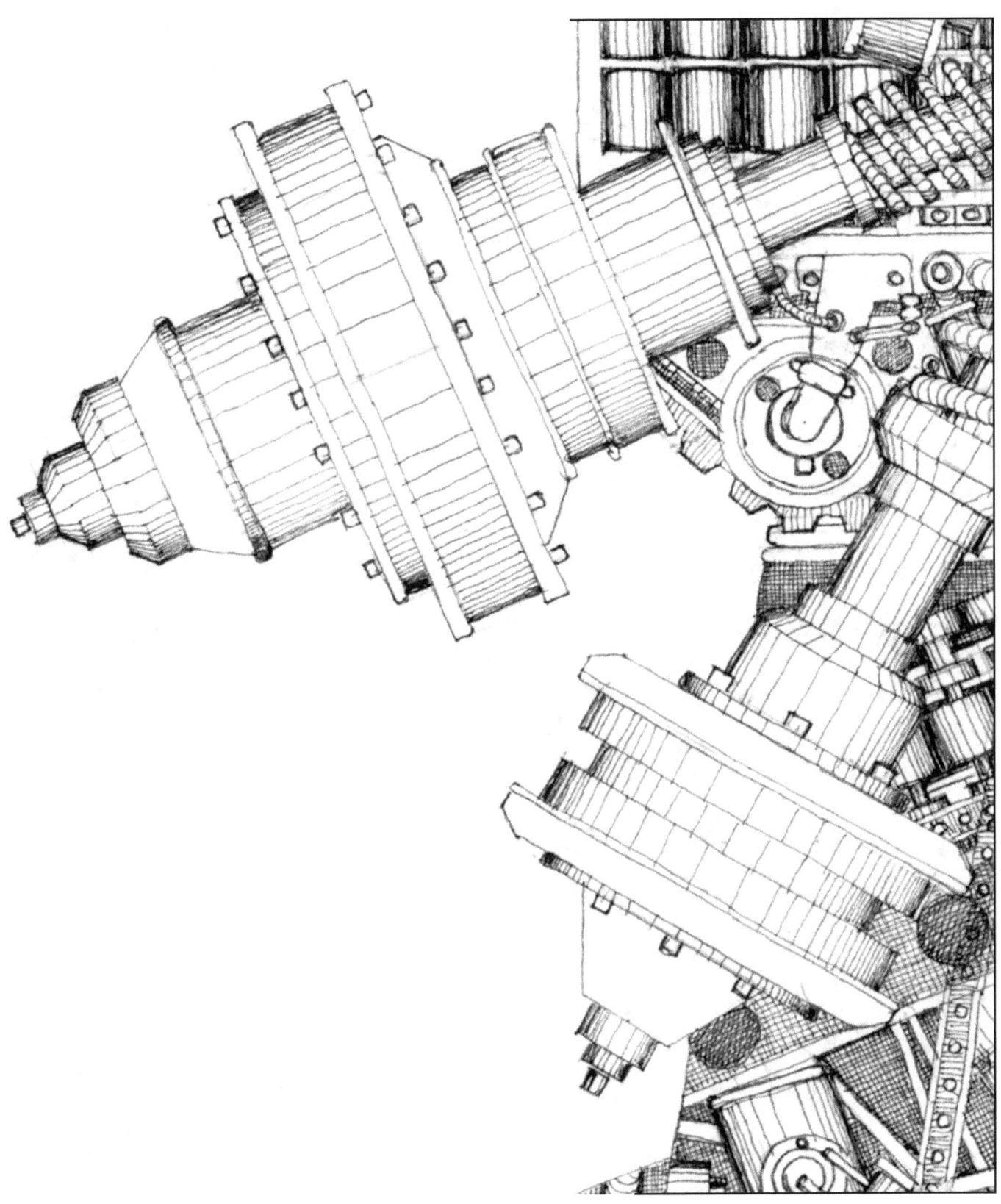

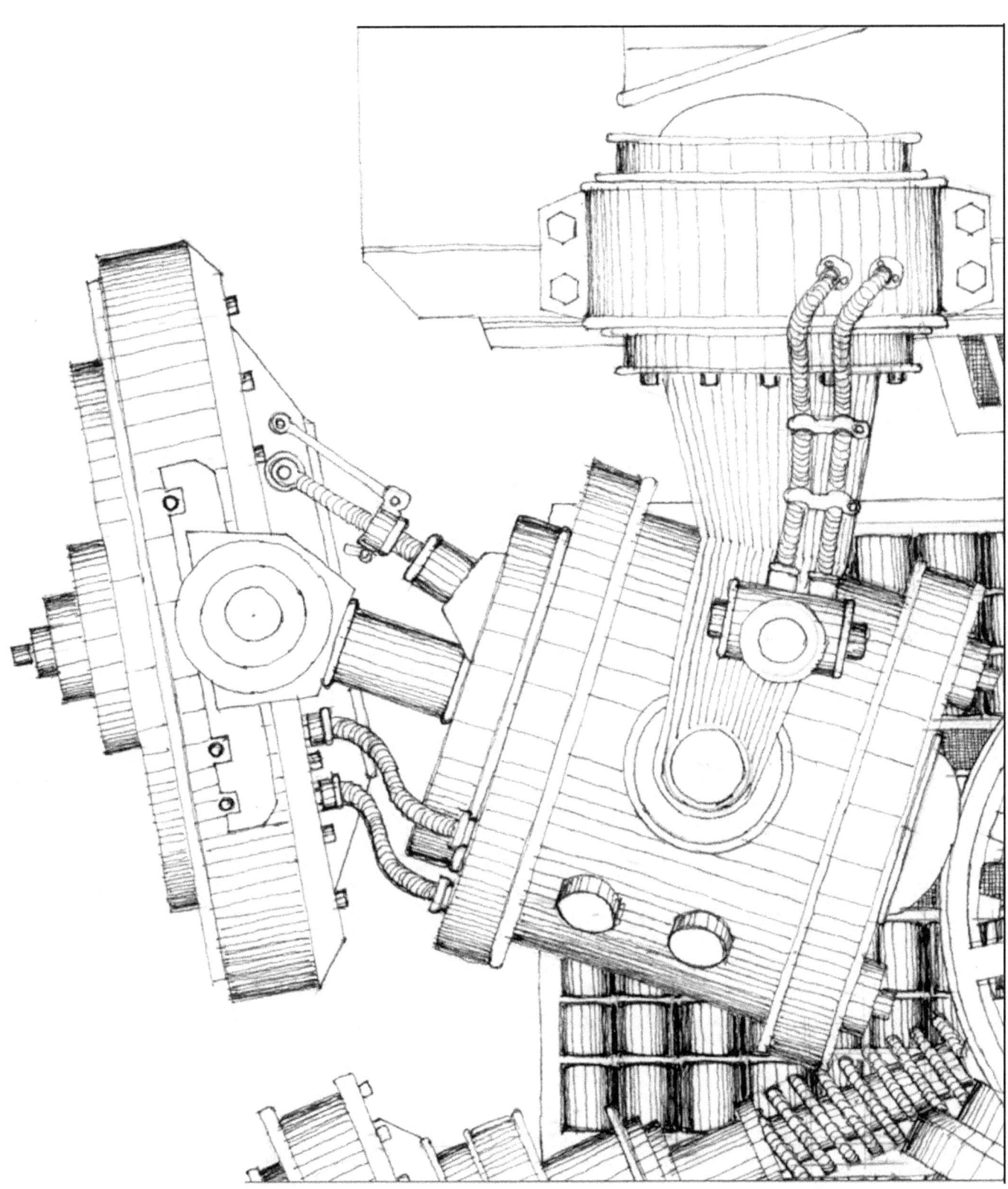

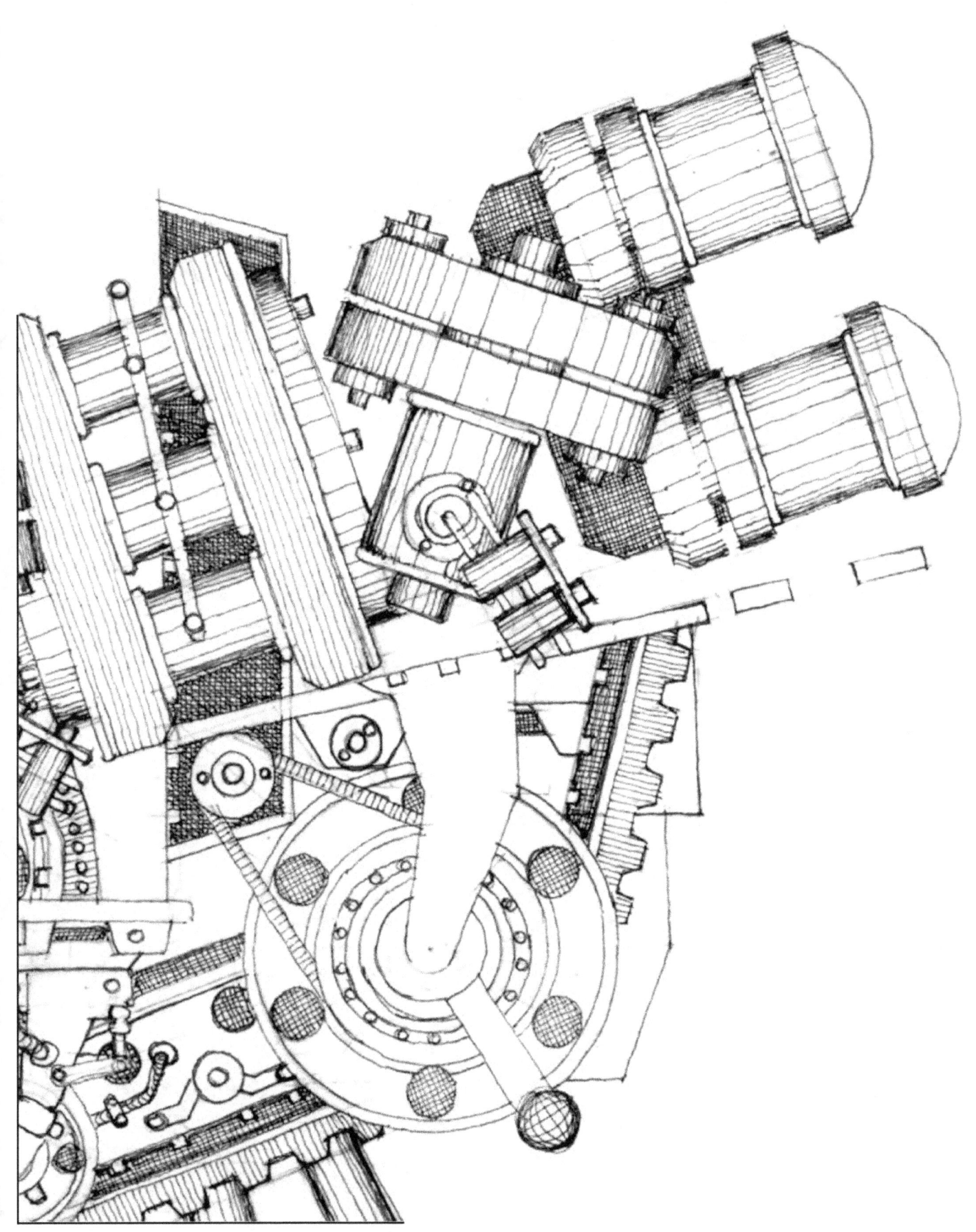

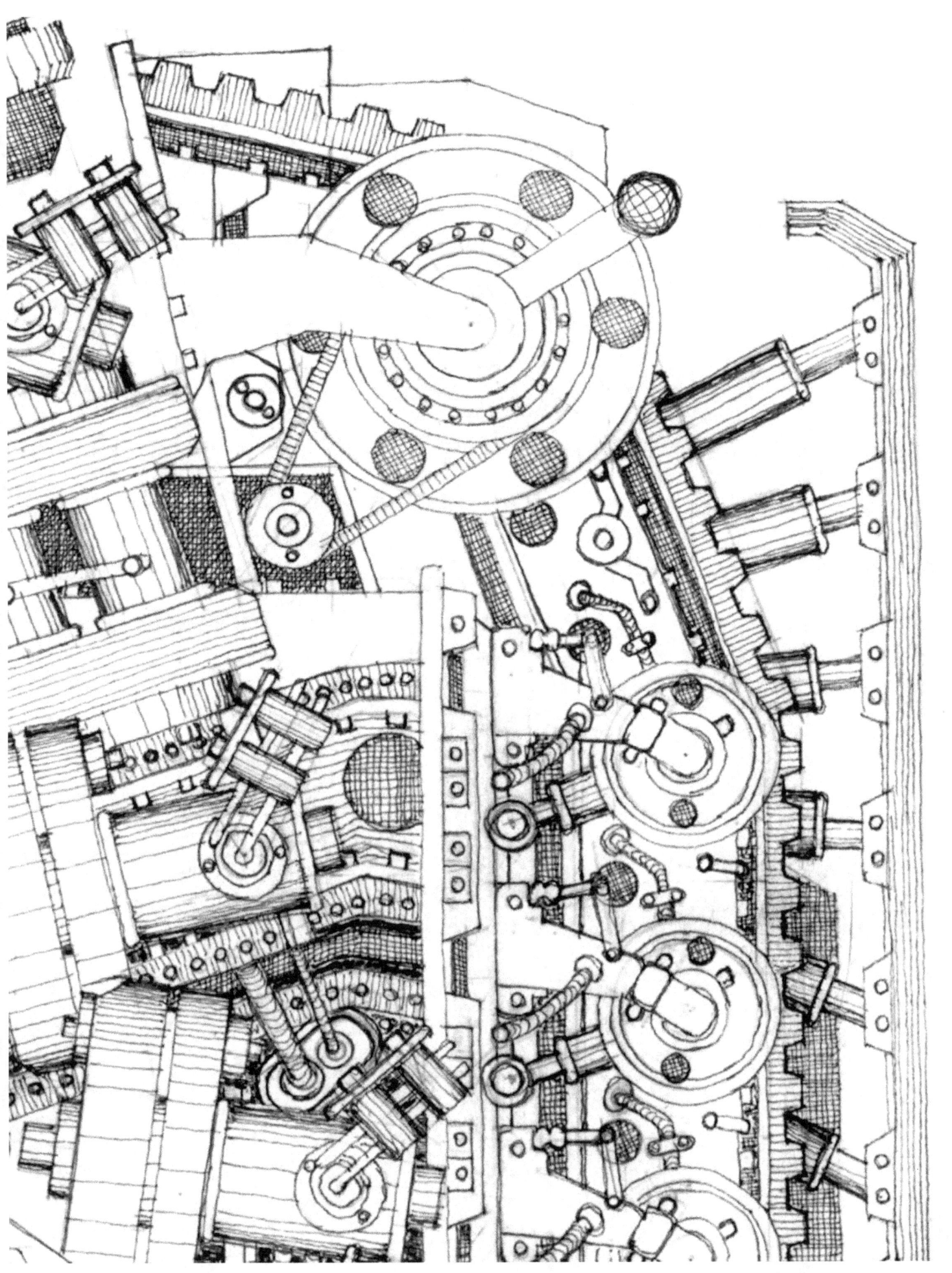

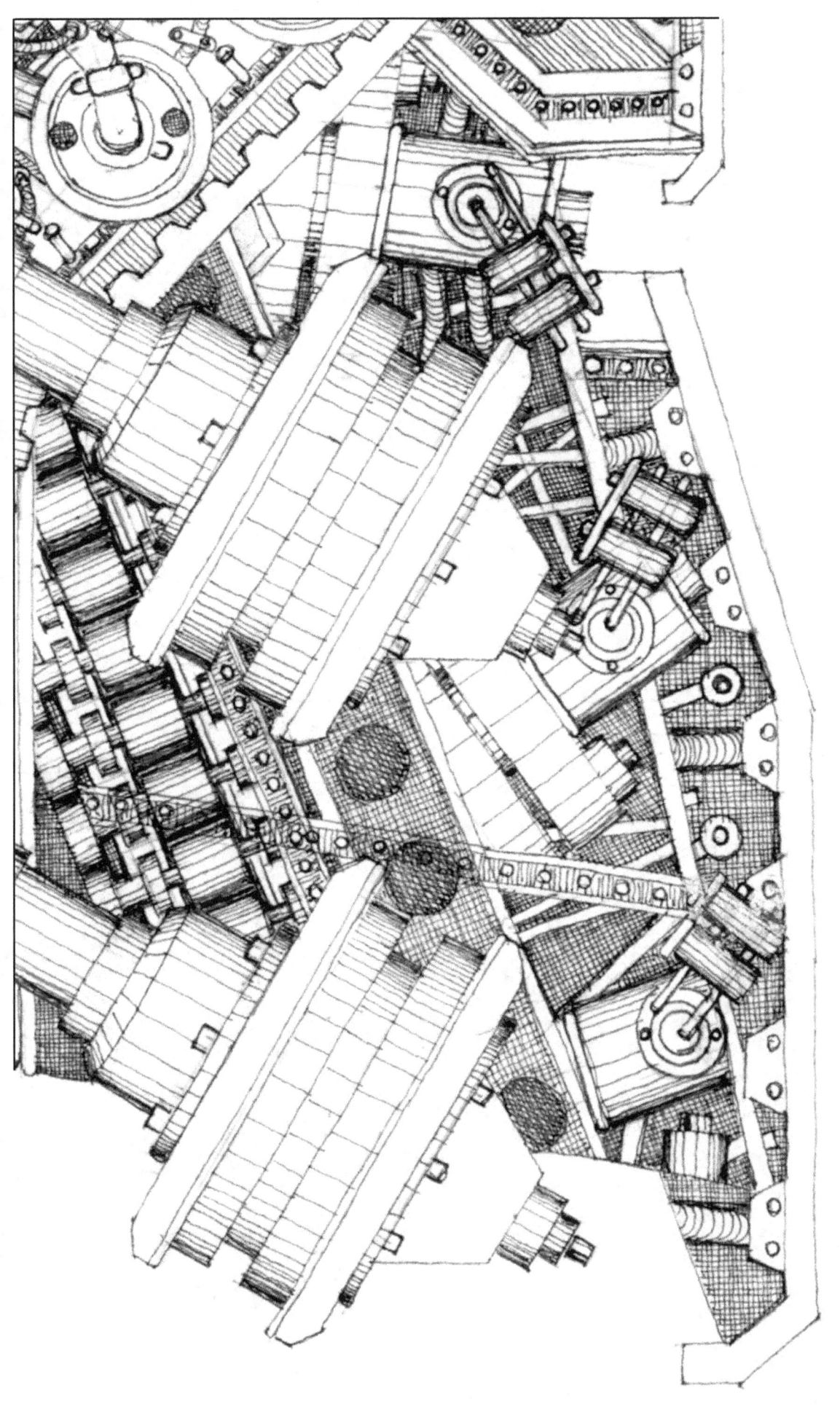

RENDEZVOUS

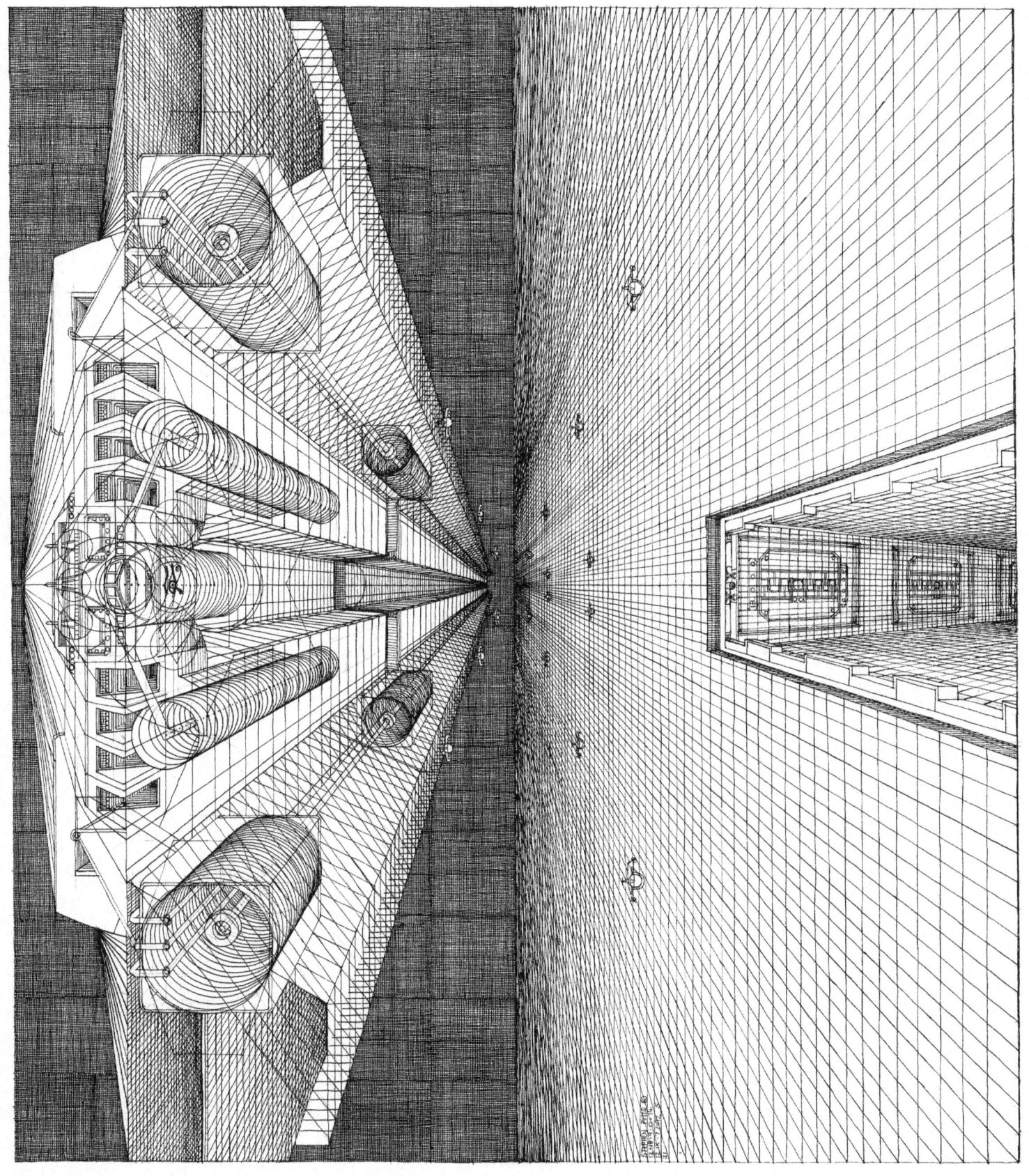

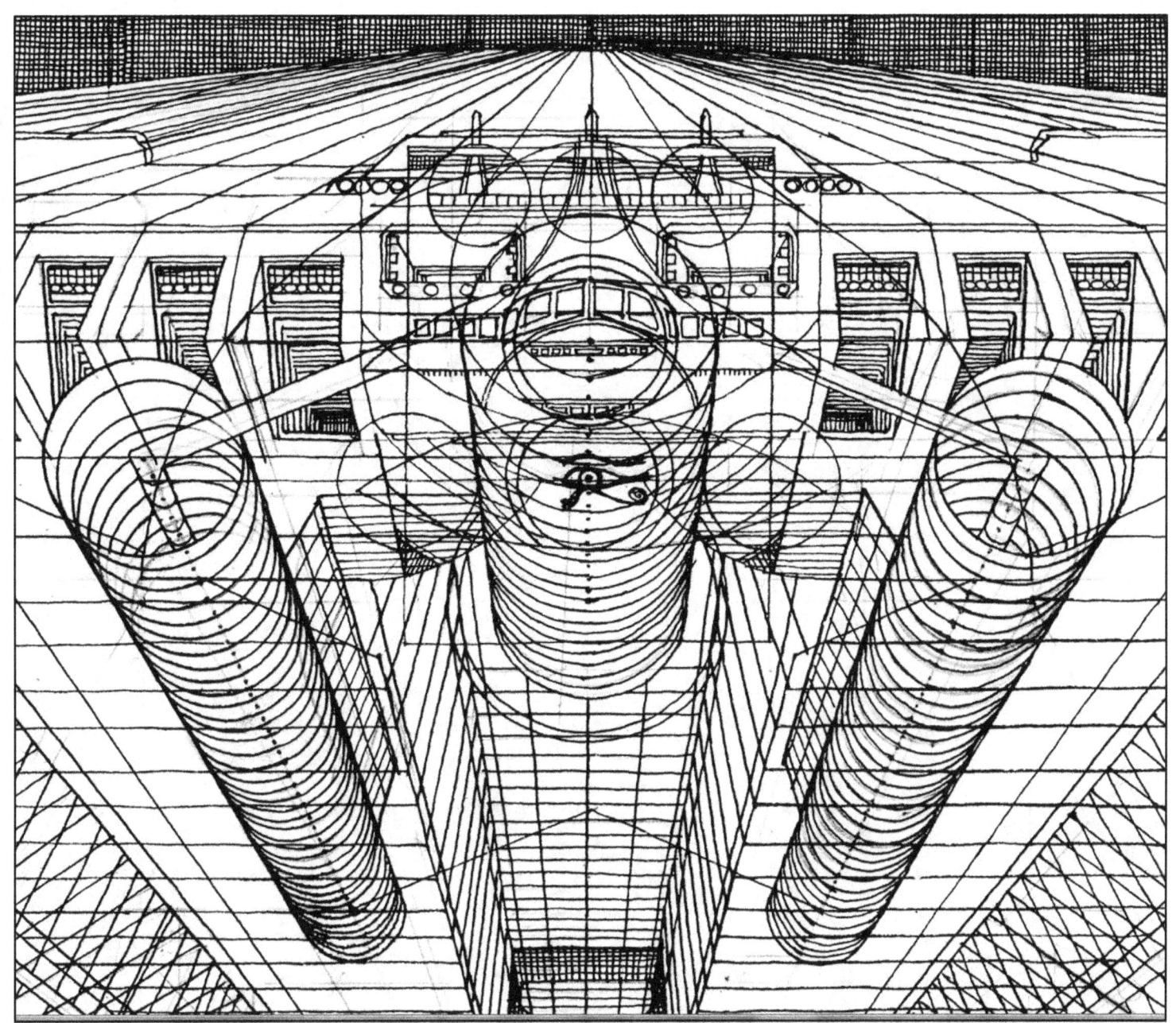

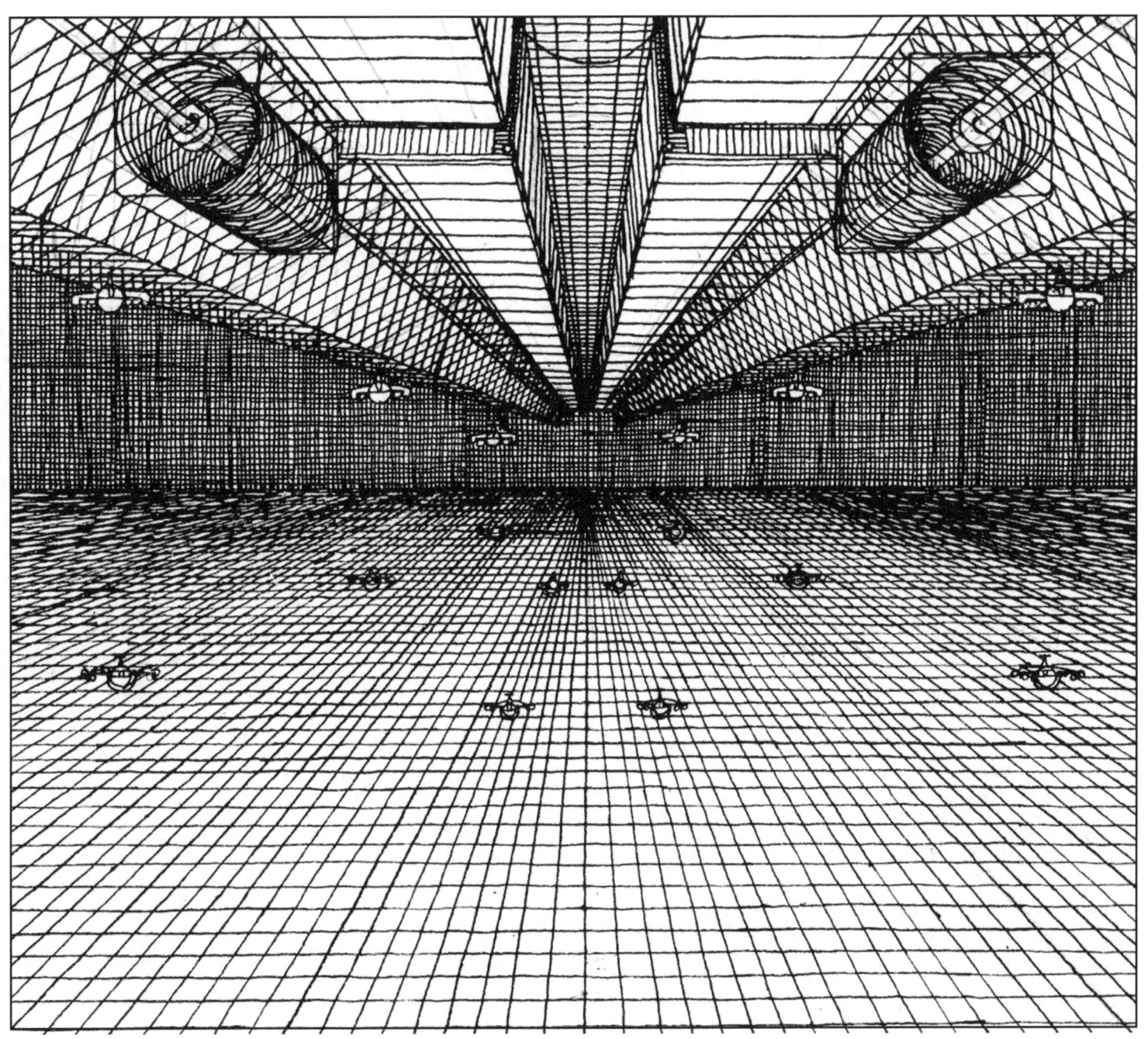

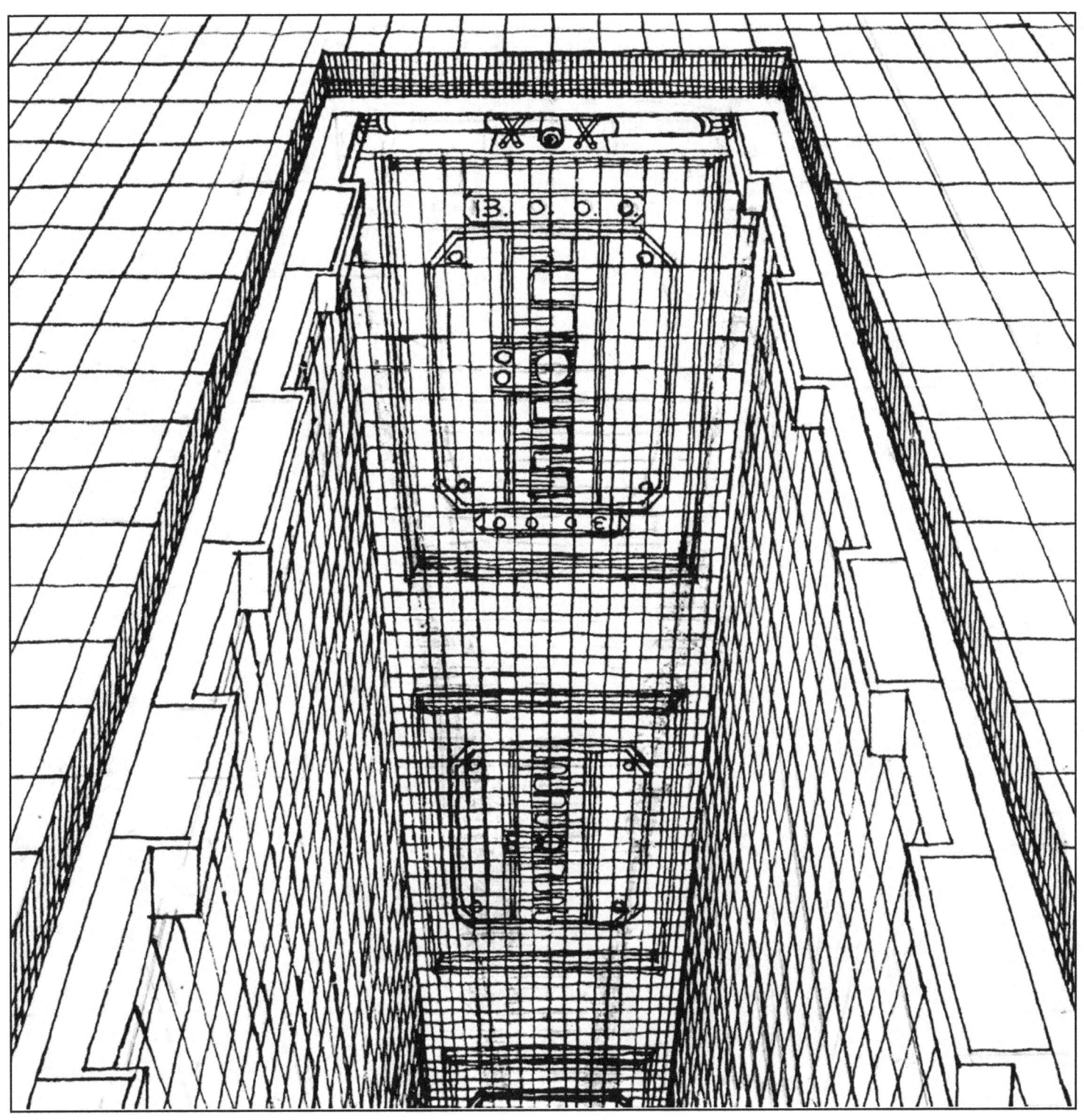

Dihedral Structure

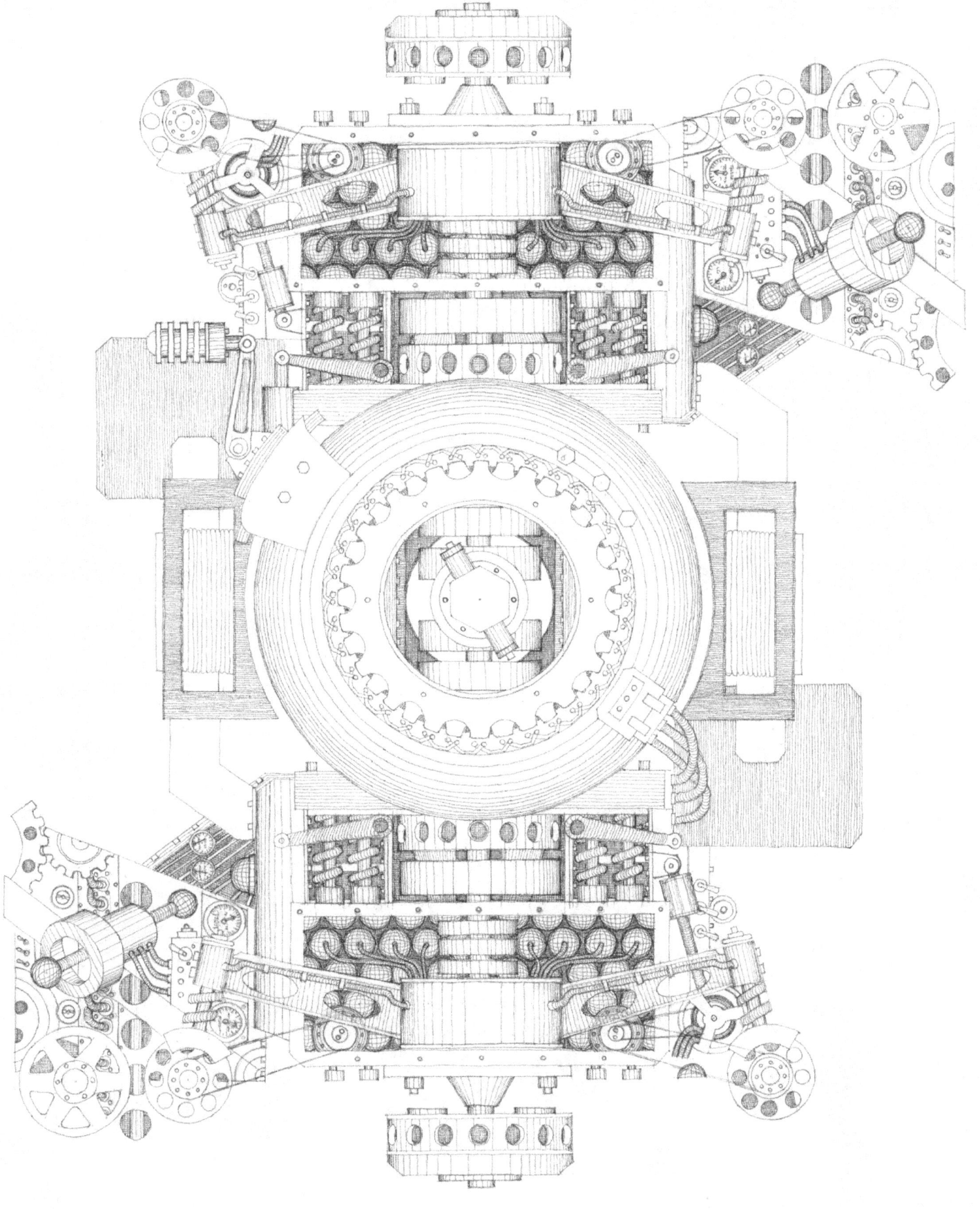

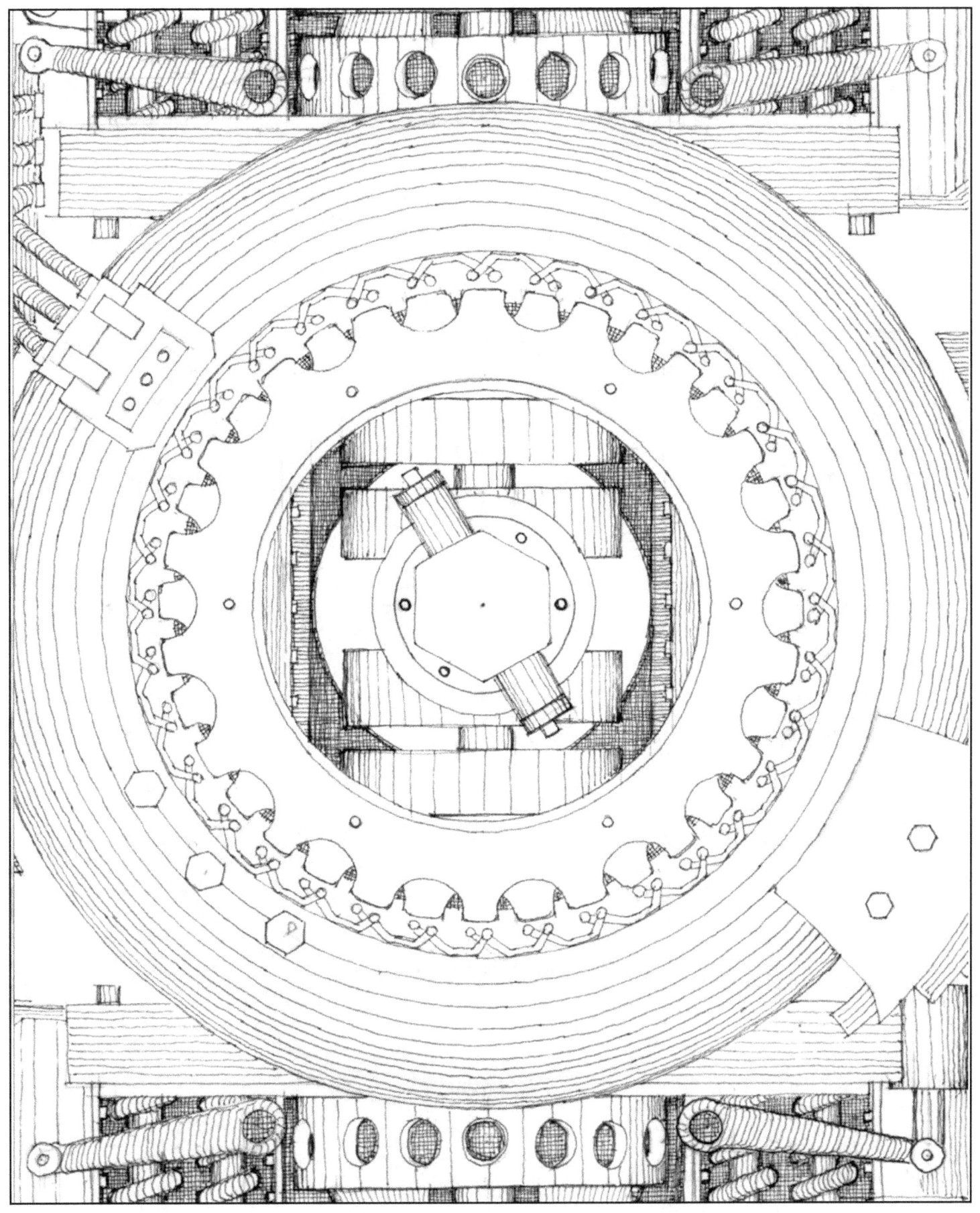

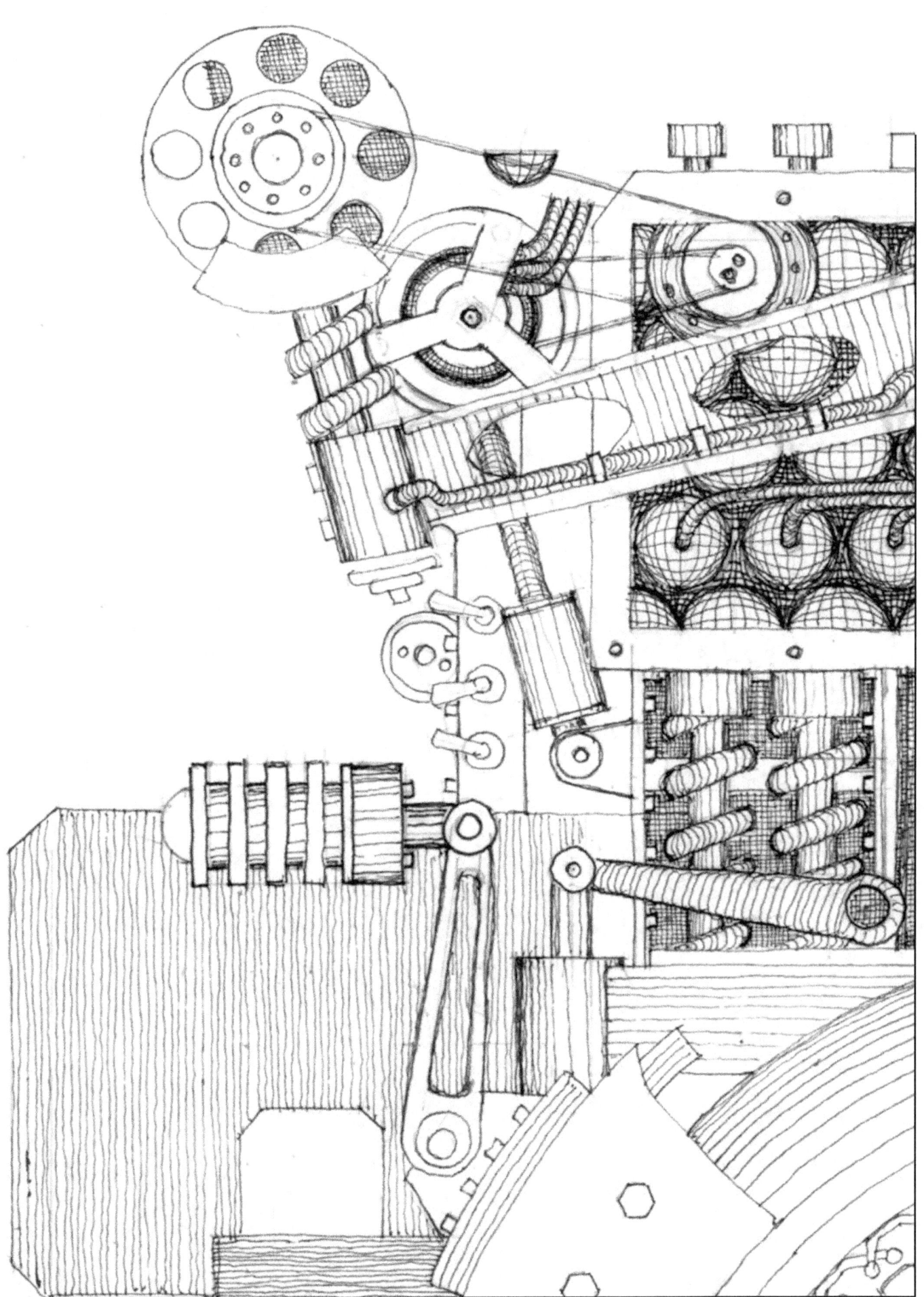

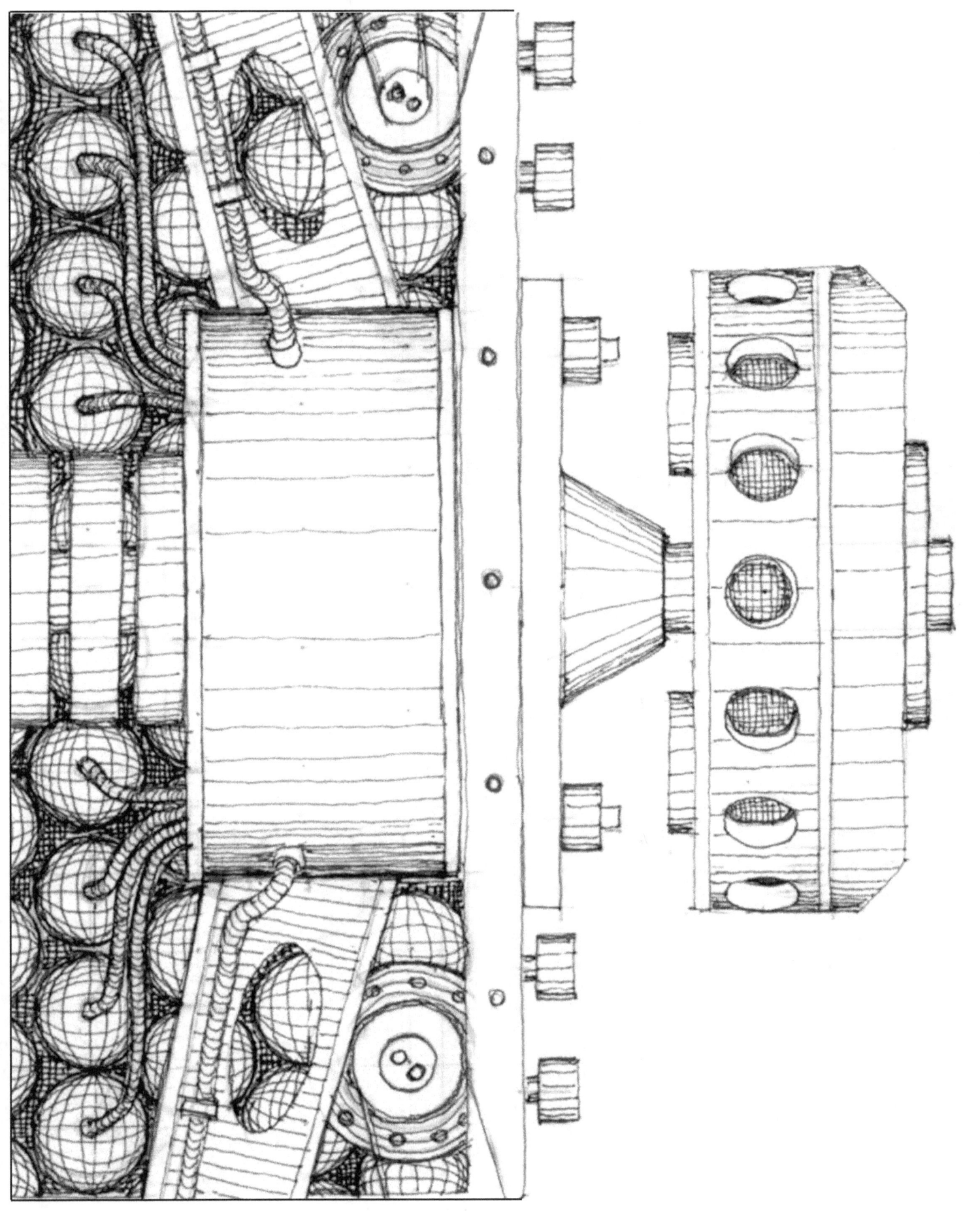

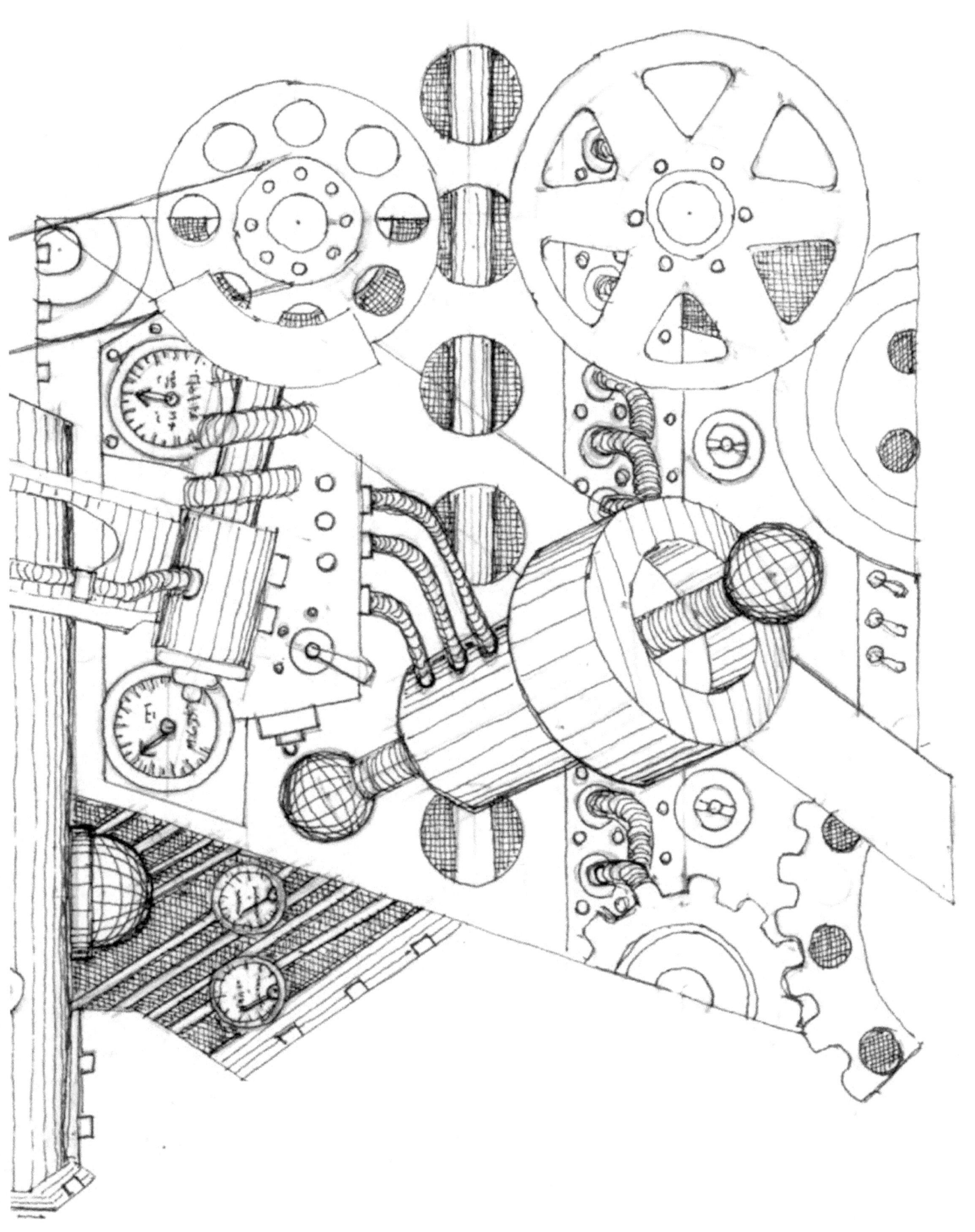

Machine

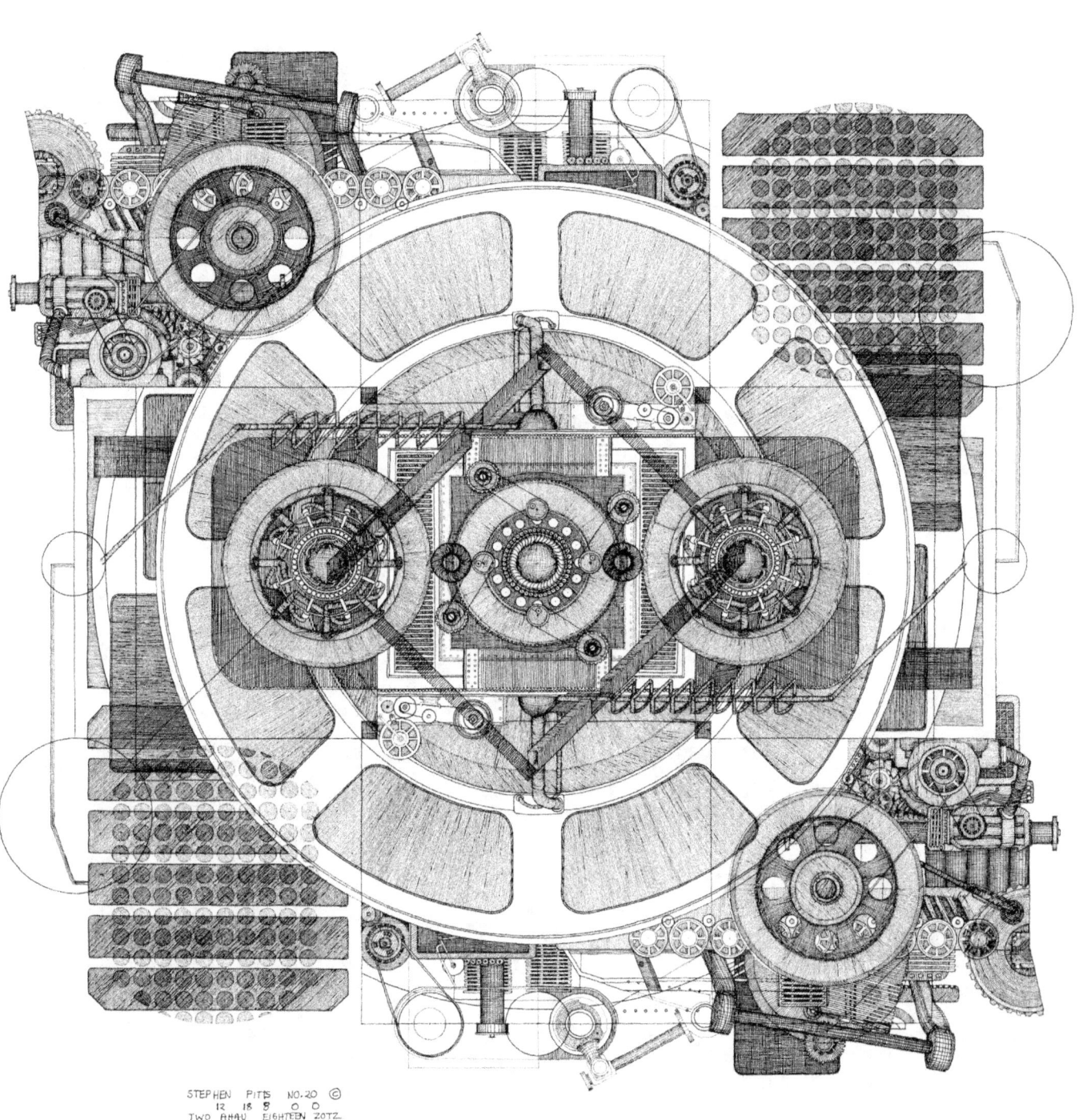

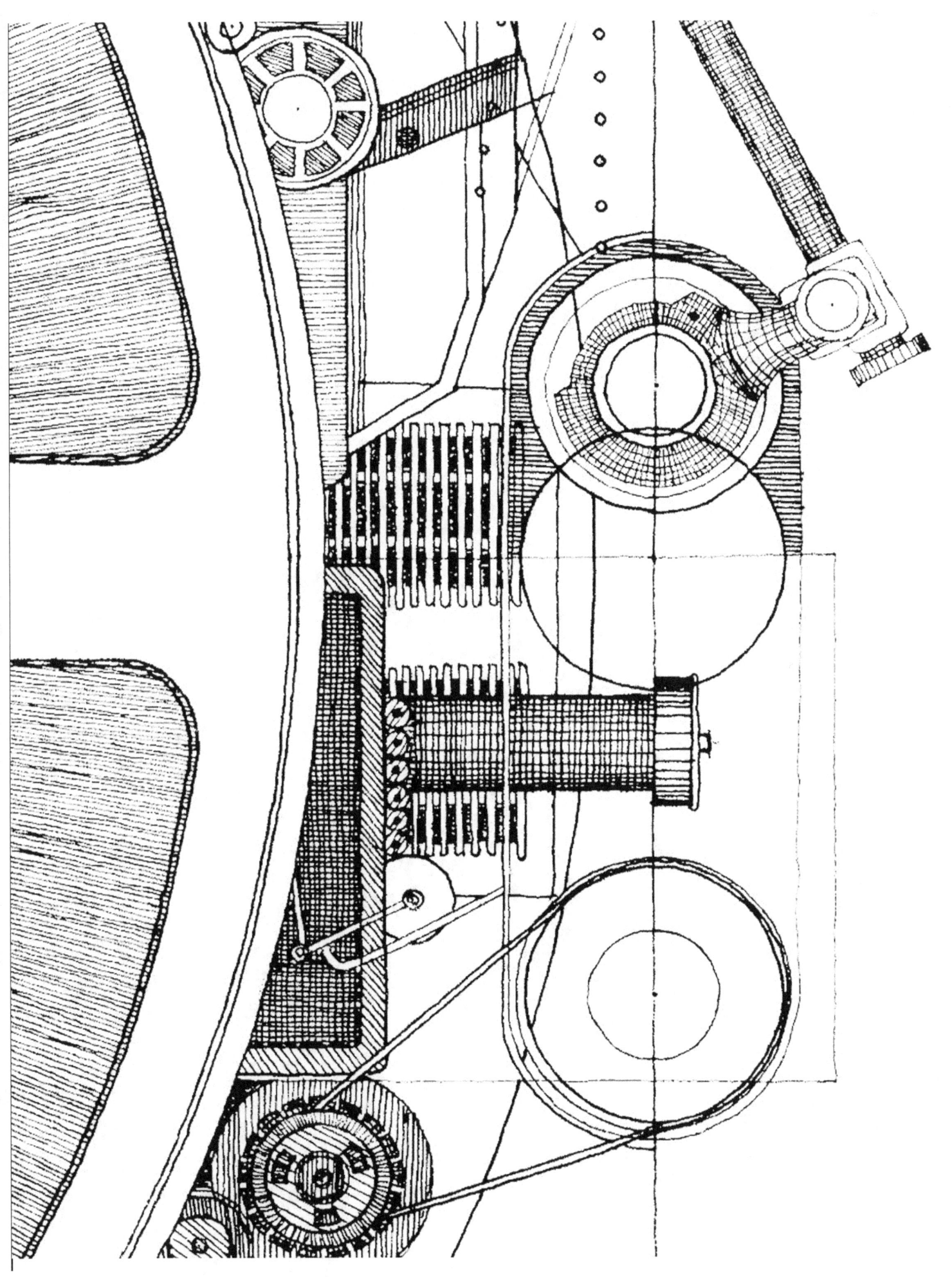

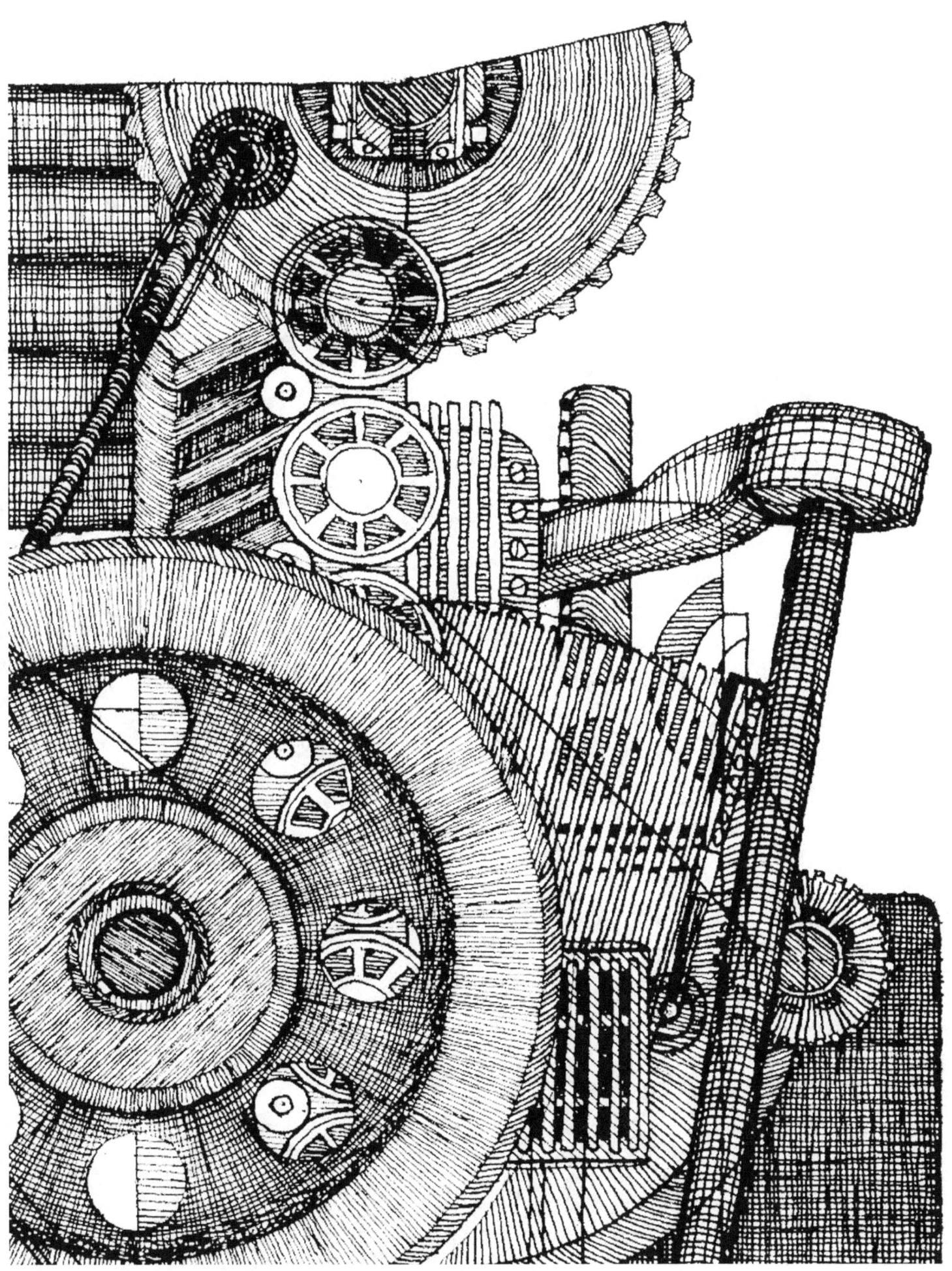

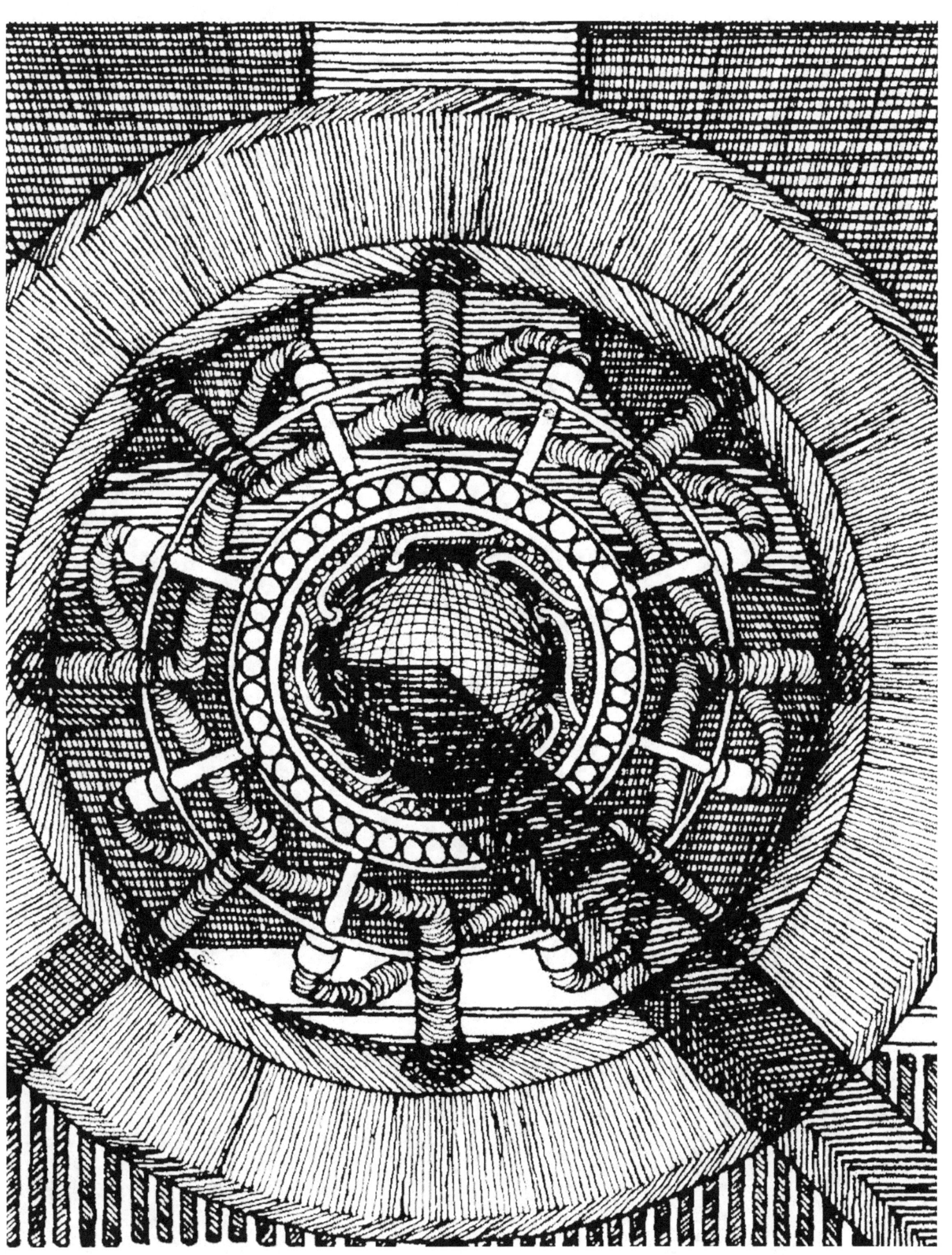

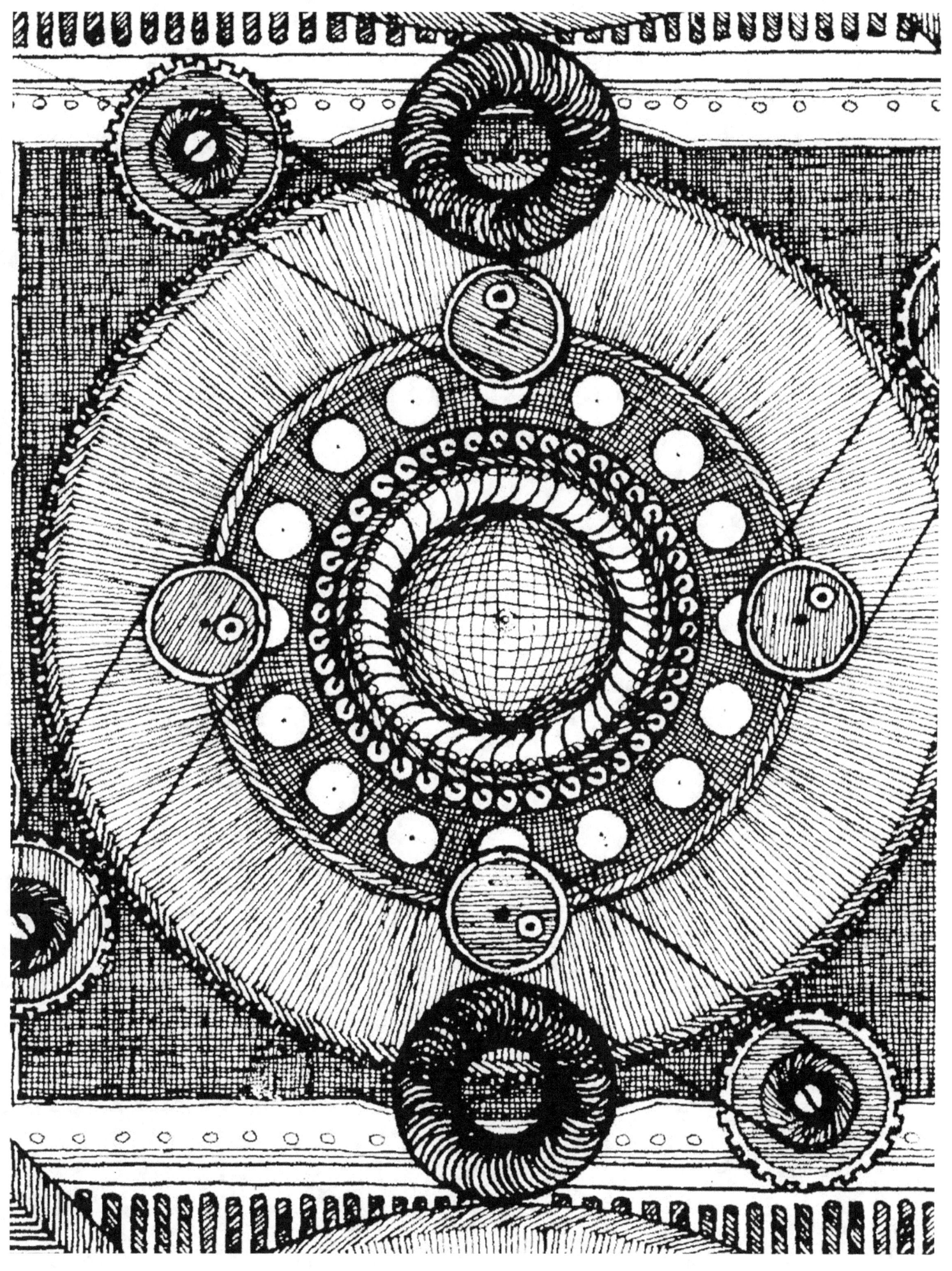

Vessel of the Quancing Grig

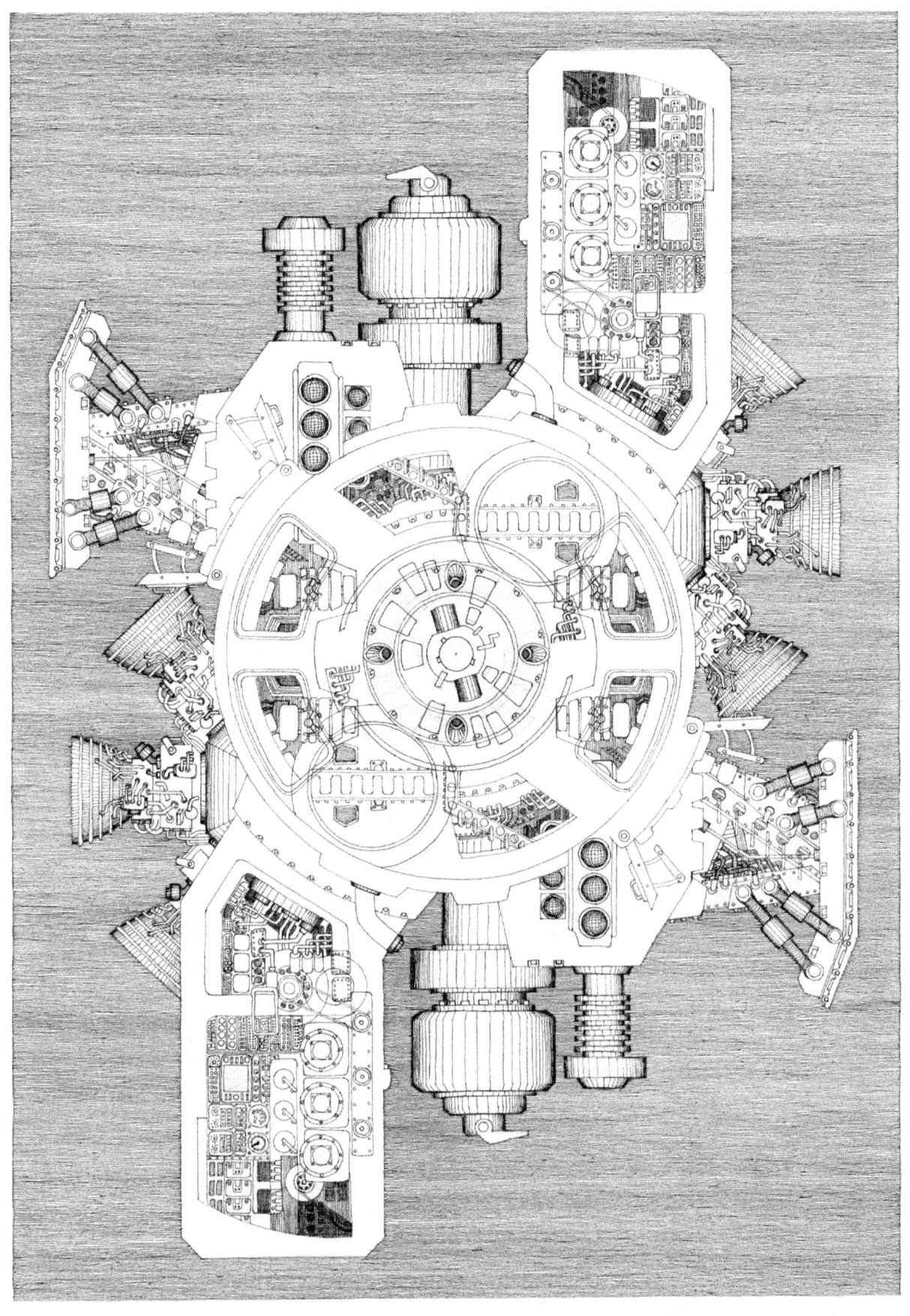

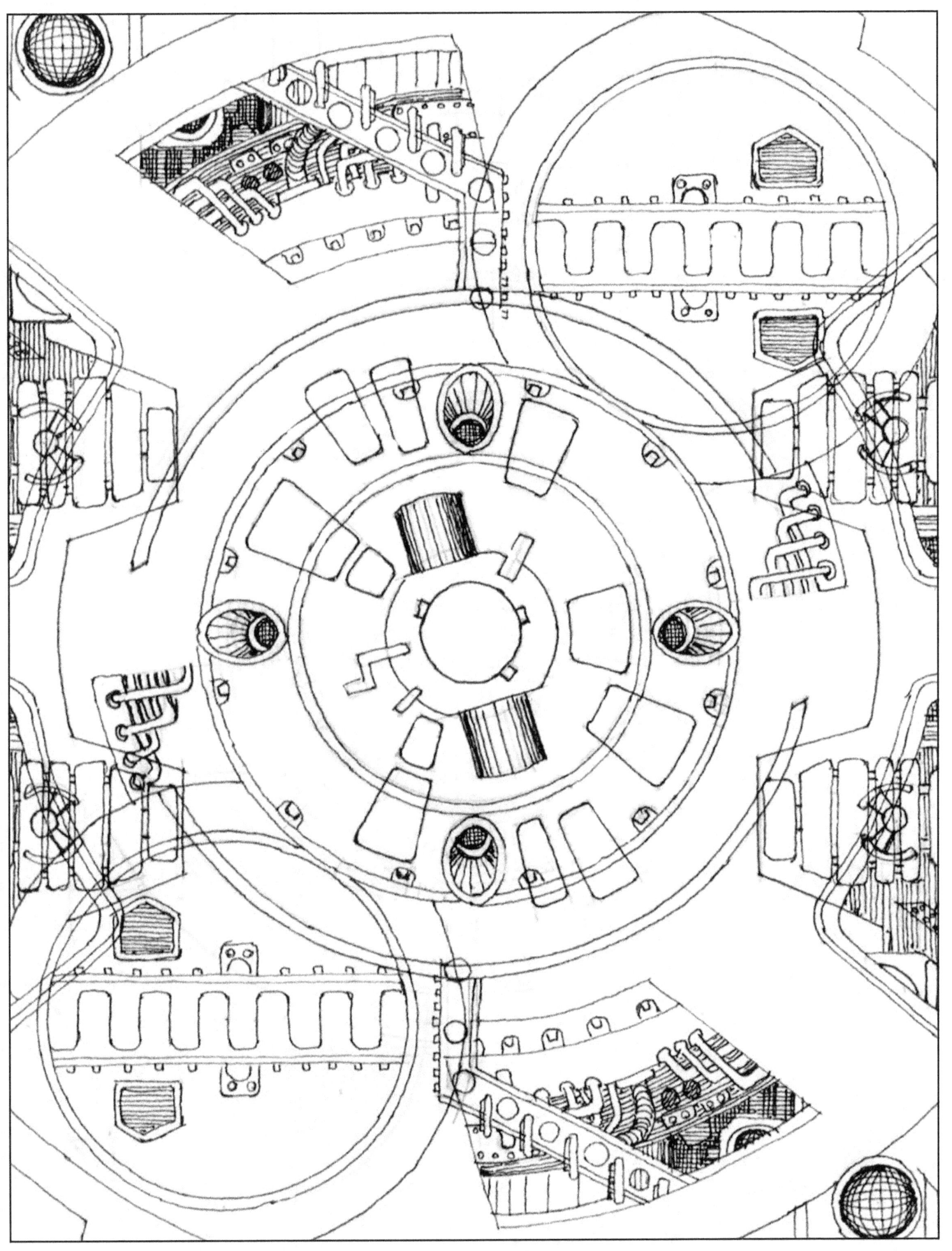

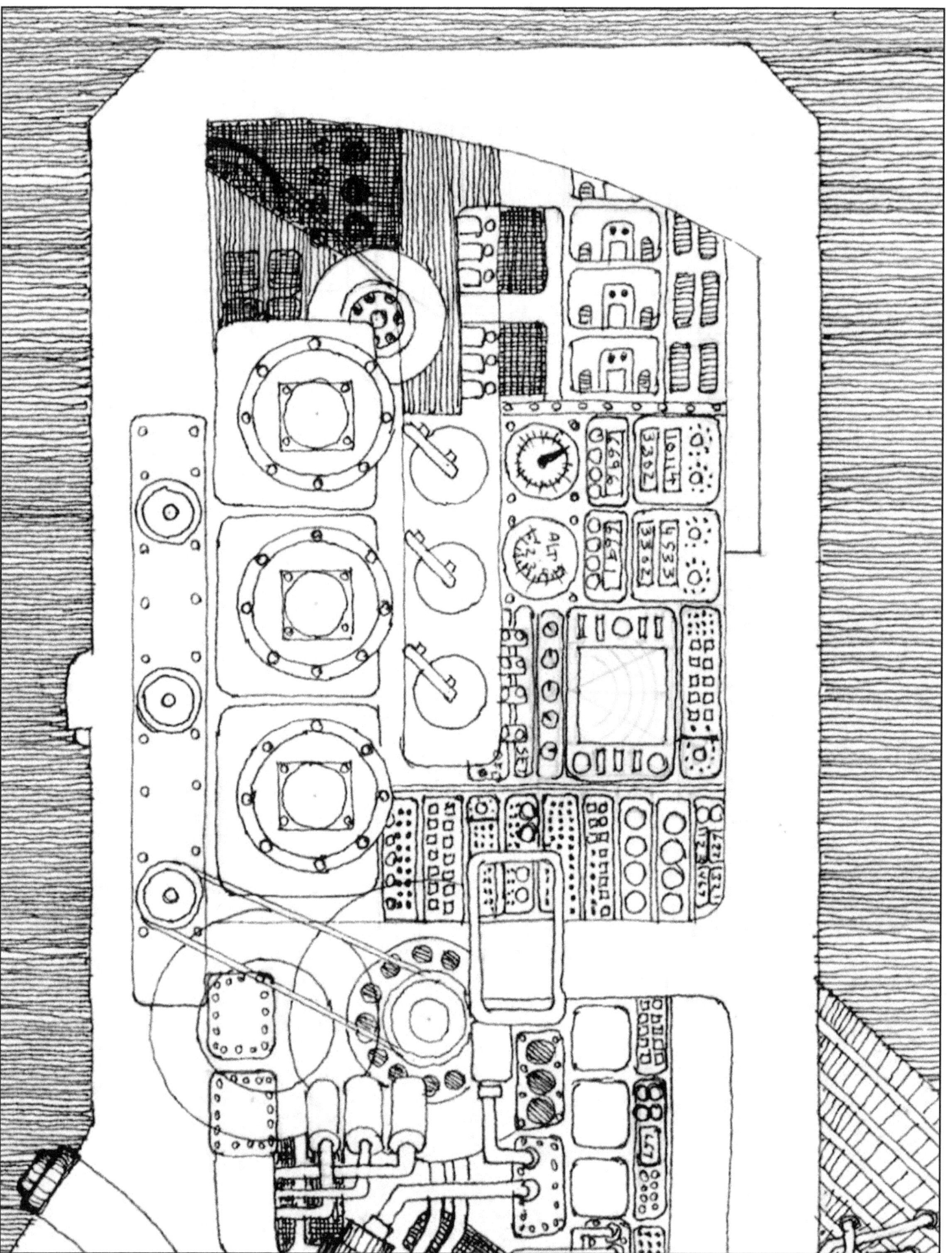

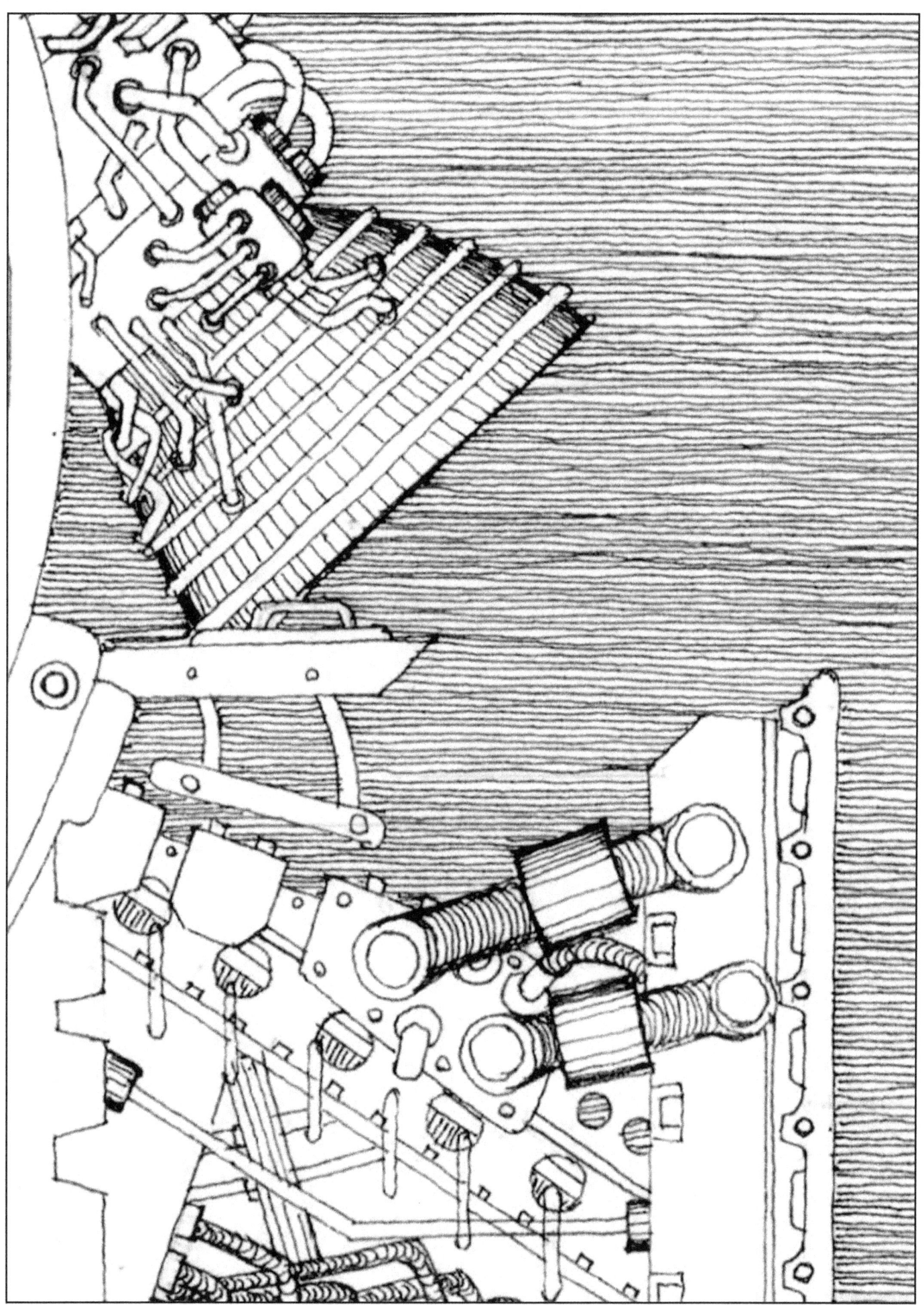

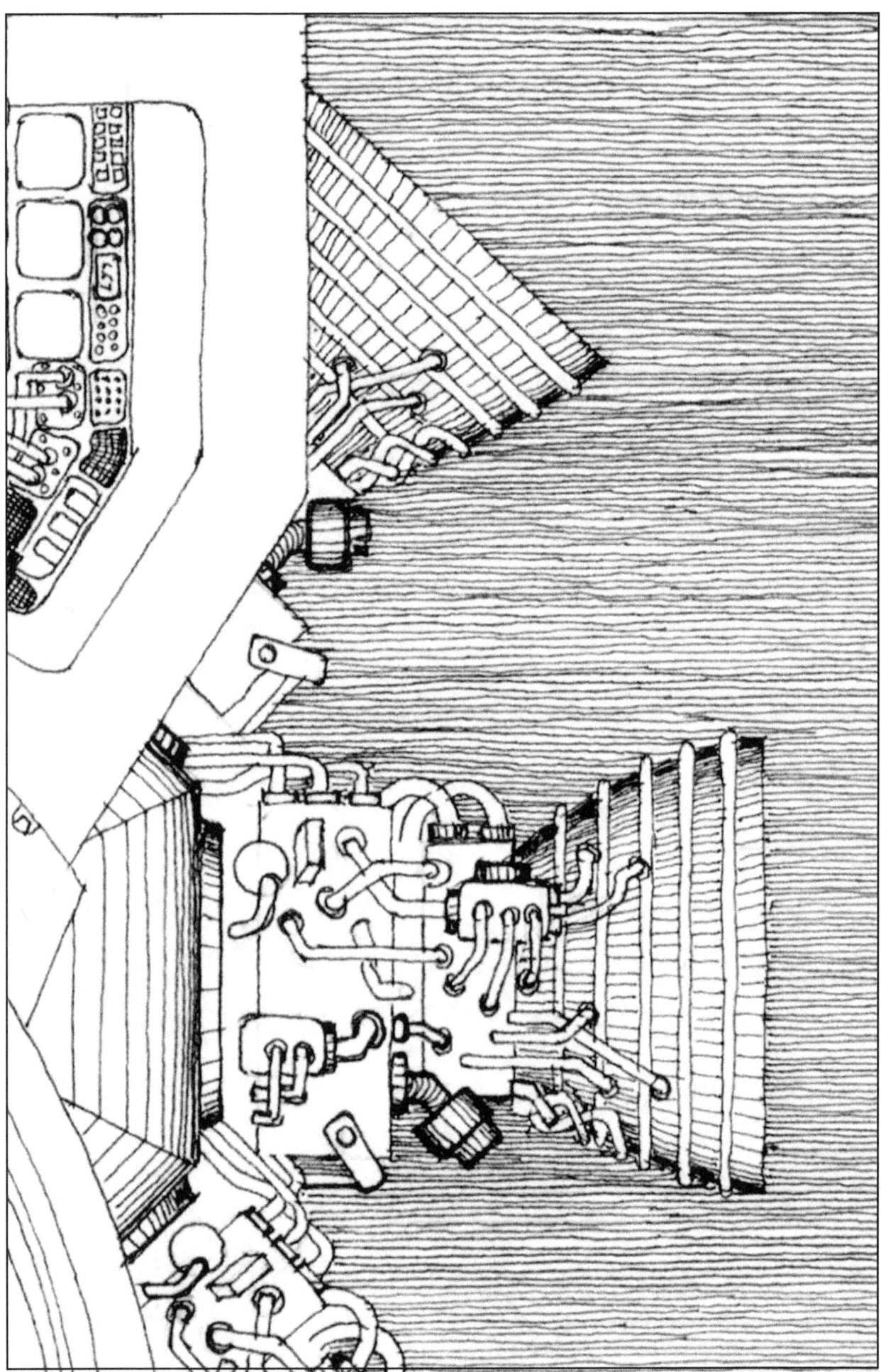

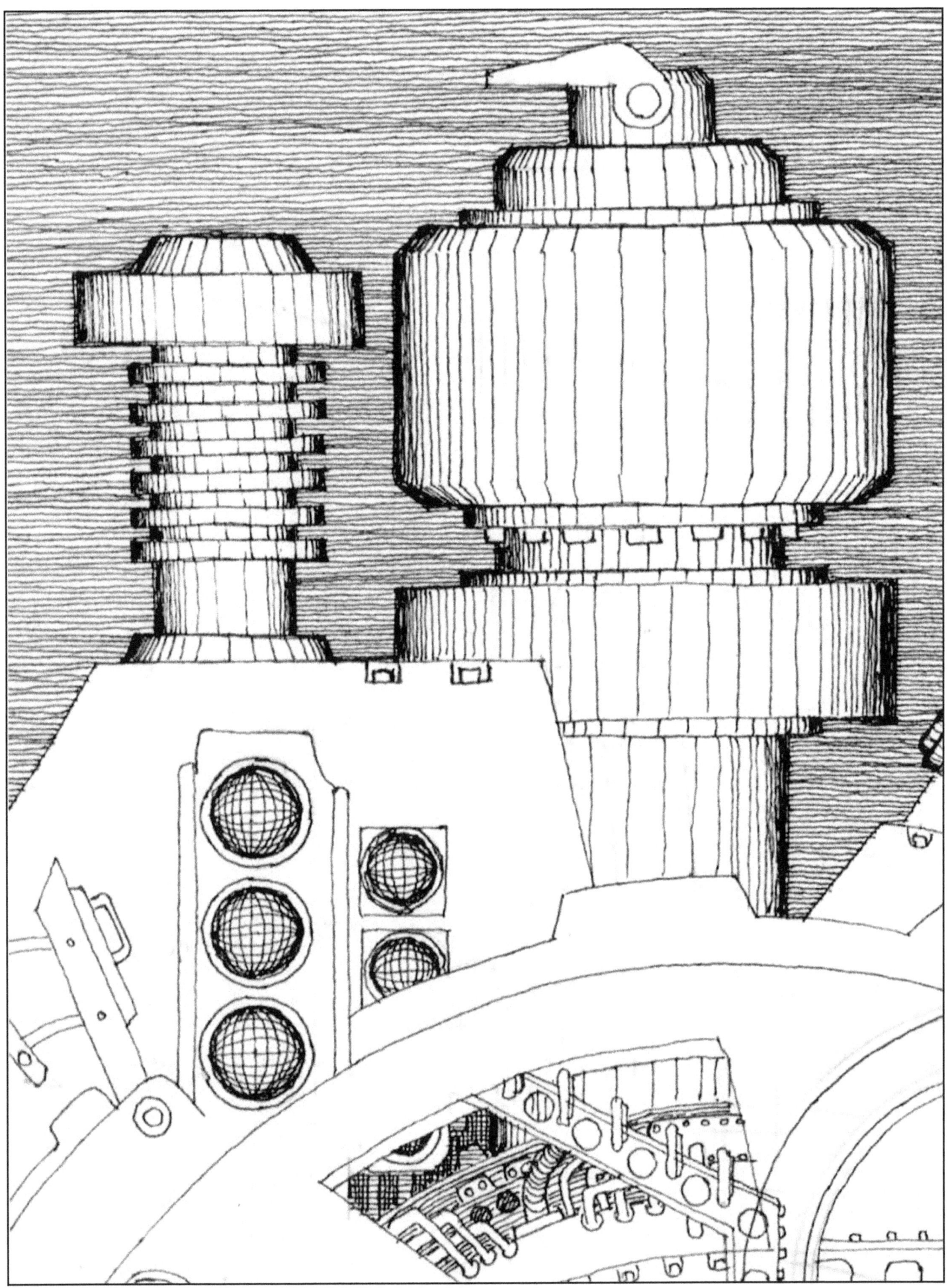

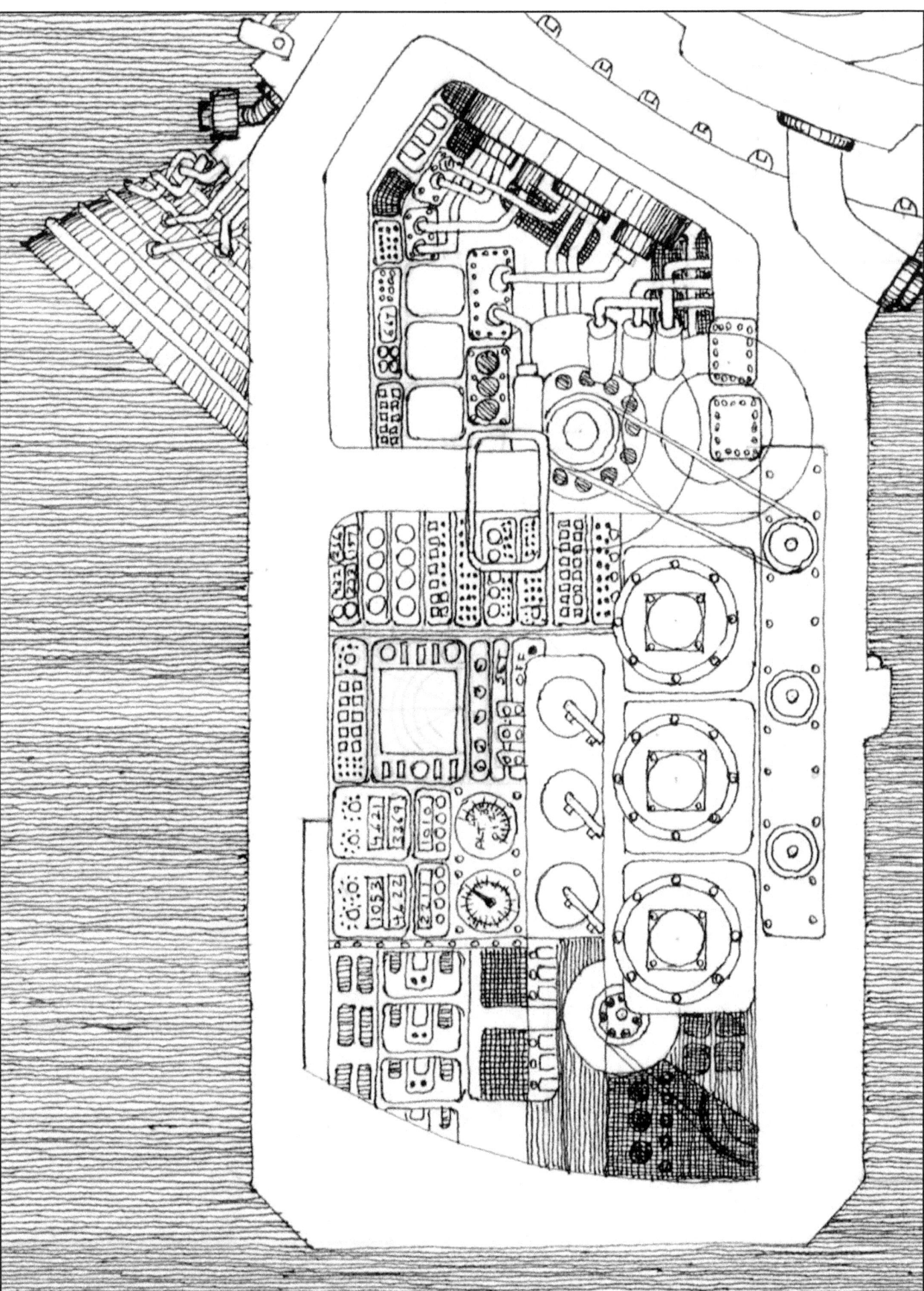

TEST PAGE

Before you get started drawing, try out your pencils, pens, and erasers on this page. Look to see if your drawing materials bleed through the back of the page before you start on a drawing you want to keep.

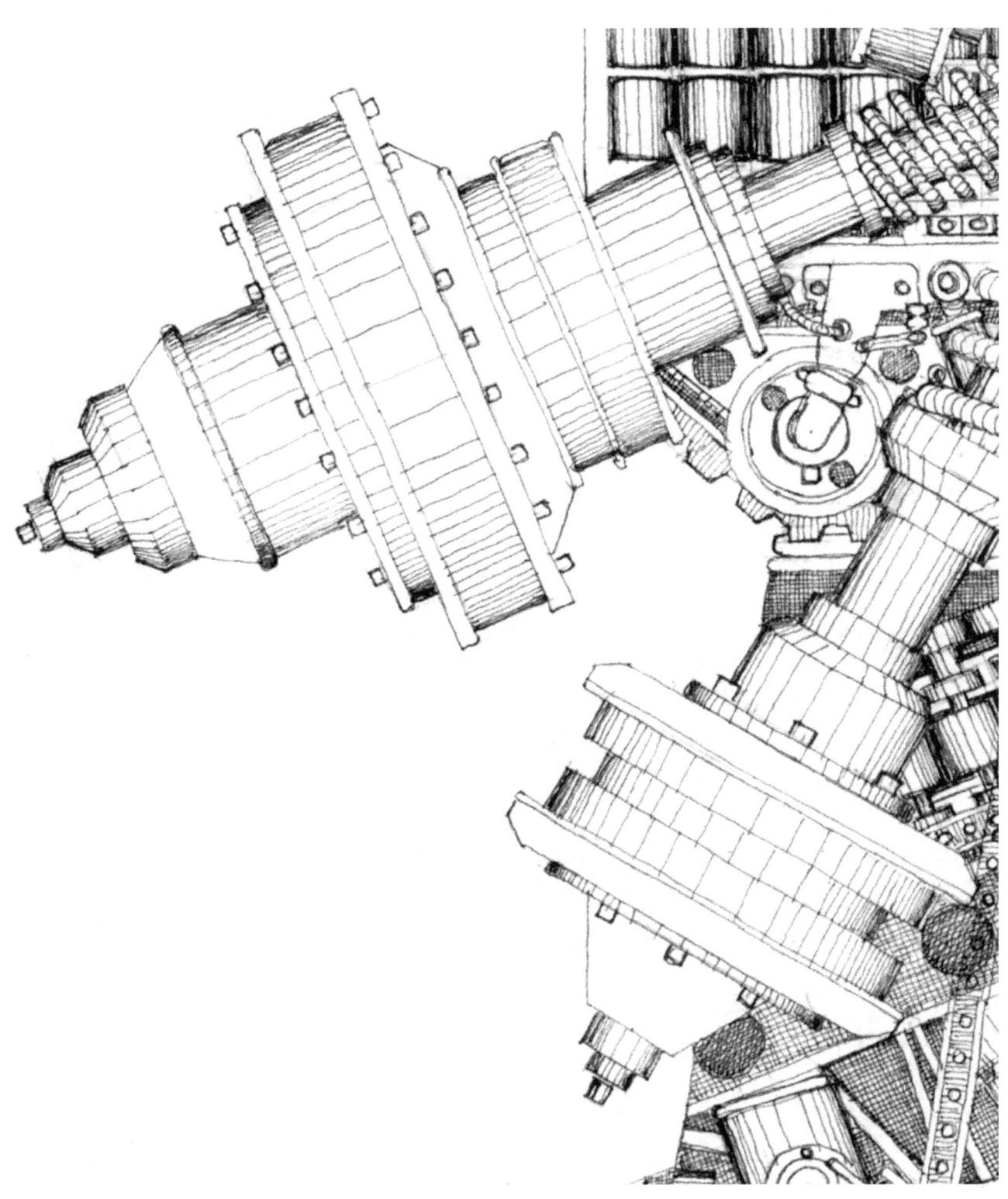